Just Like Oz

Also by George Drew

Toads in a Poisoned Tank

The Horse's Name Was Physics

American Cool

The Hand That Rounded Peter's Dome

The View from Jackass Hill

Down & Dirty

Pastoral Habits: New and Selected Poems

Fancy's Orphan

Drumming Armageddon

Chapbooks

So Many Bones (Poems of Russia)

Hog: A Delta Memoir

Just Like Oz

Essays on a Few Poet Wizards
& Their Multifaceted Magic

GEORGE DREW

Lake Dallas, Texas

Copyright © 2022 by George Drew
All rights reserved
Printed in the United States of America

FIRST EDITION

Requests for permission to reprint or reuse material
from this work should be sent to:

Permissions
Madville Publishing
PO Box 358
Lake Dallas, TX 75065

Cover Design: Randall Drew
Author Photo: Rick Kunz
ISBN: 9781956440126 Paper, 9781956440133 ebook
Library of Congress Control Number: 2022932004

In Memory of
     Paul Ruffin,
          Editor & Friend

Table of Contents

xi   Of Puffery

Wizard

1   Lodging a Poem

4   Poems that Jack Took: The Dressing Down of an Editor

14   Crazy Dance: What Actually is Being Said in Father/Son Poems

Random Wizards

27   I Beg You, Ezra

32   In the Kingdom of Babies: Galway Kinnell

34   The Name is Kumin, Not Frost

37   The Gods, the Genes and a Fire Raging in the Belly

Wizard

41   Sometimes That a Poem Is Masterful Is Enough

47   Fixing the Shimmer: The Hard Art of Poetry

56   What Makes a Poem a Master Work?

67   Up Against Time: Physics & the Poem

Oz

75   And the Flood Flowers Now: On the Trail of the First Hippie

80   Lingering Sweetness: On the Road with George

83   Just Like Oz: The Making of a Book

Behind the Curtain

91   Marble All the Way: The Poetry of Allen Hoey

132   Nude Man in the Water: The Poetry of David Dooley

140   What Students Need to Know about Syntax

142   Acknowledgments

143   About the Author

Being a poet is a funny kind of jazz.

—*John Berryman*

OF PUFFERY

Once I saw a book entitled *Just What the World Needs: Another Freshman English Text*, or something to that effect. I easily can imagine someone reacting likewise to this book: "Oh, dear, another book of literary puffery!" Why, then, risk it? I'm not an essayist of any note—no Lewis Thomas, Loren Eiseley, E.B. White—nor a fiction writer the likes of Sherwood Anderson, Raymond Carver, J.D. Salinger. I know I'm not precisely because I know and love the work of these and others of their pedigree so avidly. They're full bred; I'm mixed, which has its benefits. Call me a double whammy. Whereas I can't aspire to their elegance of style and thought, I can to a tenacity that's mine and owes no allegiance to any but my own gut feeling, genes and mental grasp. Why this book? The work exists, that's why. It's mine, and I wish to let you in on it. And that's as close to noble as I get. The rest is skin and blood and bone: I'm damned tired of first having to locate and then lug around in a bulky black binder all these pieces when I want to read them to an audience, as I sometimes do. A single slim—and I do mean slim—volume is much less strenuous, thank you. It's really that simple. Still, since it also will exist, I hope you find some pleasure in this book. If so, that's good; if not, who knows? There might one day be just what the world needs: a *Puffery II*.

Wizard

Lodging a Poem

Famously, Emily Dickinson said that she knows a poem is a poem when it makes her hair stand on end. Fair enough, but then again, can't a poem that isn't a poem produce the same effect? Alas, like Prufrock's hair, at least on my crown, mine is growing thin. So much for Dickinson.

Seriously, though, as a writer, where exactly a poem comes from, and how, was, is and always will be a mystery, at least to me. But that's beside the point for this little exercise in which I'm engaged. The mystery I'm interested in pertains to the reading of poetry, not its writing: Why, I've always wondered, does a specific poem in a collection of generally fabulous poems stick to one's memory like a barnacle to timber, never to be dislodged? In other words, why that one poem and not another?

Take this poem, "Imagination and the Man" from *The Collected Poems: 1971-2011* (NYQ Books, 2011) of Jared Smith, a Colorado poet who probably isn't known widely but ought to be:

A falcon landed in the apple tree outside my window yesterday:
a bird of the sky and high telephone poles, that would not act like this.
Yet he sat there, focusing the small leaves and twigs around him,
drawing the whole vast structure of the tree into his intensity.
Until in the end there was nothing but his eye that I was looking at;
all else moved around it as fog moves across a meadow.
I sat on the sofa facing him, not six feet and one pane away.

It would be foolish to say I think that we were matched
or that we were bound together, but it is true that time binds and we were
    there.
Had either of us moved, the surface would have broken, mirrors shattered.
It was a touch of magic in my home, empty of people and filled with life.
And then it spread its wings, tangled briefly in the tightly wound limbs,
and was gone. I will not sleep tonight, nor for many more.

There you have it, thirteen lines split between two stanzas, one of seven lines, the other six; this brief lyric, from a book that contains many other more major and longer poems to choose from. Yet this small gem has lodged itself in my memory where, as Frost so wittily said, it is hard to get rid of.

So why?

There are, as anyone might expect, many reasons, and at some risk I am going to elaborate—risk, because I want to write an essay, not a review or a critique. Like the poem, then, I will force be brief.

Briefly, there is its brevity: Falcon lands on apple tree, man sits on his sofa "not six feet and one pane of glass away" watching the falcon watching him, man muses on time and his and the falcon's place in time, man decides the moment is a "touch of magic" in his home, falcon spreads its wings and after tangling them in the limbs is gone, man loses sleep.

Not very difficult to remember, this plot, such as it is. But of course this is a poem, and what matters is what the poet makes of such a miniscule moment. Smith makes much. For one thing, there is the sheer lyricism inherent to the situation: the falcon itself, the natural world of apple tree, its leaves and twigs, the conjured image of fog moving across a meadow. For another, there is the identity-splintering metaphor of mirrors shattering, and the symbol of the falcon and its transforming, nearly transcendental eye.

All of these contribute to the pull this poem has on me. So does the simple grace of language; that felicity of expression only a seasoned poet like Smith can achieve, what is in effect a linguistic maturity: "It was a touch of magic in my home, empty of people and filled with life." Indeed there is magic, and not just in his home. Magic is in his poem, too, as both the pattern of stress and syntax of this line reveal: the iambics of the first part of the sentence giving way to mostly dactyls in the second; the definitive statement that is the main part of the independent clause, the modifying material that is its appendage, not to mention the paradox of an empty home that's filled with life.

So there's all of that, too. And then there's the mastery, the elegance, of those long lines spreading out across the page, much like the falcon spreading its wings, readying itself for flight, this final observed action in perfect concert with the poem readying itself for closure. The arc, the trajectory of the lines mirrors perfectly that of the man's imagination.

But this is an essay, not a review, remember? So, before anyone emulates the falcon and takes flight, and as with any smartly structured essay, the major point I wish to make I've saved for last.

Smith makes much of this encounter, I've said. And so he does. But I'm not talking just technique and language and structure. Again, Smith *makes* much, and what he makes is exactly that which we are privy to—*the making*. The poem doesn't present itself as a fait accompli. We get to see, literally, the imagination at work, beautifully so. It shapes the experience into a poem shaped by the experience. For me, this is the real allure of the poem. Basically, in a very intimate way, we are allowed in. We are in that room, experiencing the man's imagination making of a falcon something more than just a falcon. What I find so irresistible is the intimacy. The man is imaginatively open to the world and therefore naked before it, his aesthetic and moral compass on full display. Sharing it as we are, so are we. The man is enraptured by a raptor, and so are we. This shared intimacy, this binding of the man and the bird in time and space, and through the poem our binding to them, our imaginations to the man's, transforms us, connects us to both kinds of nature—human and natural. Beauty and Truth? Oh yes, those, too, but even more to art; that is, in this case, to the poem.

So there it is. What attracts me to this particular poem, what leaves its poetic imprint on my memory, is, above all, its mystery, its magic, which is the mystery and magic of the imagination. Like those tightly wound limbs entangling the falcon's wings, the poem binds me to itself, won't let go, flight in this case that very binding, ever the paradox of art, ever the sine qua non of memorable poems.

For Emily, what marked an inescapably profound poem was her hair standing on end, and I assure you, when I read Jared Smith's "Imagination and the Man" whatever hair I have remaining *is* on end. But for me, what marks a poem as special, what separates it immediately and forever from any number of other amazing poems, is expressed by Smith in the final line of his poem, when he concludes: "I will not sleep tonight, nor for many more." Neither will I. That's how I know.

Poems that Jack Took: The Dressing Down of an Editor

So there you are, at your computer hunched forward and reading through another batch of the hundreds of poems that have come to you courtesy of the internet. By now you're bleary-eyed and wondering how it is that everybody, or so it seems, thinks they're a poet. How did this come about? You can remember, back in the day, when you could rattle off the thirty or so literary journals everybody wanted to be in. Now there are so many no one knows exactly the number. Like crocuses in spring, they pop up, flower for a brief spell, then disappear, others as quickly taking their place.

But today there is no one to take your place. Wearily, you open another attachment, start to read… Then you sit upright, startled into ambition. The first poem is a revelation, a gem that sparkles with everything you value in a poem. Quickly you read the other four poems in that batch, and almost instantly choose one more (space and format being what they are). You have a pair. Not that you have voiced the specific reasons for your selection, but you know—you *know* the reasons, instinctively. But objectively, too, you know.

Welcome to the world, as I imagine it, of the contemporary editor fueled by love of literature and no doubt countless cups of coffee—a world of long hours, blurry eyes and minimal funding. No doubt, too, we poets curse and condemn editors regularly over slow response time, near misses, outright rejections, and in general for the poor state of every literary Mouse-that-Roared kingdom on the planet. We dress them down as a mitigation of frustration, of an always impending sense of failure, of helplessness. And, as news folk are fond of saying, in the interest of full disclosure, I too am guilty as charged of all the above.

Recently, though, Jared Smith, a good friend and a poet whose work I much admire, emailed me good news: Out of a batch of four or five poems a certain editor, first name Jack, had accepted two. This left me wondering: Why those two? Would a different editor have chosen the others that Jack rejected? Would still another editor have chosen one of the accepted and one of the rejected? Would another have accepted all of them, and another rejected all?

The laws of probability suggest the answer to all these possibilities is Yes. For each, all it takes is the right editor at the right time. More interestingly, though, is what an acceptance can tell any alert enough writer about what that editor values in a poem. Certainly this applies to Jack. A close reading of the two Smith poems he accepted reveals his poetic predilections clearly, which is to say, specifically.

Here are those two poems:

He Does What It Takes

Curling his finger around porcelain
he cradles the morning cup of coffee and watches
steam rise between his fingers, how each finger
shapes the fog of morning with his unique mark,
his DNA and his fingerprints upon the swirl of time,
and he listens to the tick of the clock upon his wall,
the first birds beginning to sing in his garden,
and a dog startled by dawn down the street,
the morning paper hitting with a thud at his door.

This is what the man is before he goes out
to turn the ignition in his family car. It is what
his wife thought of before she thought of diamonds
and before there were other souls beneath this roof.

It is the little things that make the man what he is,
the scent of his chemical balances, the colors he sees
as sun rises over the blasted buildings of his city,
the tiniest bits of the universe that have come to him
and pulled together to be unique in all of time.

This is what he is, and he goes out each morning
to do what the machine asks and comes back each night.
At night the crickets are calling to the darkness and light
within him, and the hum of commerce fills his veins.
He whispers of love with each breath he takes.

Rivers Will Flow

So much snow has fallen while we slept
the spring crocuses now bloom beneath a blanket of ice
and are warmed enough for the melt that will come.
The tulip and daffodil shoots also losing their green
retain their green beneath the balance of all colors
and their roots will fill themselves with the water of time.

Wake up, lazy head. We all sleep at our own time.
It has snowed so much while we slept rivers will flow.
Your breasts are cherry trees in a ceramic urn.
My hands remember them… my fingers urge their nipples.
Wake up, wake up in your giving of life, in your time
where all the shadows have fallen into memory. Wake. *

Probably what first registered with Jack about these two poems is that they are, clearly, companion poems, even if not intended as such by the poet. Thematically, they both focus on identity, balance, time and, each in its own unique way, love. They both are personal lyrics, yet narrative, too, and they both center on sleep—specifically, its aftermath. That is, they are early morning poems. Each is an aubade.

In "He Does What It Takes," a poem told from an omniscient point of view, we have detailed a husband's morning routine, from the moment of his "cradling [of] the morning cup of coffee" to his departure to "his city" where the "hum of commerce fills his veins"; in "Rivers Will Flow," told, in the first stanza, from a first-person point of view (established by that plural "we"), followed by the second stanza's shift into a direct addressing of "lazy head," the "you" of the stanza. Here, too, it is morning, the husband or lover chiding his loved one to waken. In both poems the morning is presented as a time of tranquility and reflection.

Similar, too, is each poem's focus on the natural world, though only fleetingly in "He Does What It Takes," in which domestic and urban imagery contrast with birds singing, a garden and a dog. "Rivers Will Flow," while more physically and even sexually intimate in its details, stays rooted in the natural world, both literally in the first stanza and metaphorically in the second—"Your breasts are cherry trees." Even contrast provides balance.

Ironically, then, the pairing of the poems, their balancing, reflects the theme of balance—and its opposite, the disjunction of the urban and the rural, the personal and the impersonal in "He Does What It Takes." Certainly this tells us something about this editor's predisposition, right from the start: He likes a clarity of theme and a development that is compelling; he likes the lyrical delivery of those themes (through point of view and imagery); and he values narrative, even when it is, as in these poems, more a narrative of psyche than any external action. He loves the lyrical, but he craves more than just emotion, more than sensory experience, more than pretty. Implicit or overt, he craves real character revelation, whether interior or external.

All this said, however, let's be even more specific. Specifically, there are three qualities that mark these two poems, and Jack's savvy as an editor: one, an intimacy of not only character but of the setting within which the character is operating, and being operated on; two, a pertinent and vital structure that heightens clarity, logic and drama; three, an absolute control of language and literary technique.

Central to "He Does What It Takes" is a fundamental ambiguity, which is established subtly in the first stanza, then develops and deepens in the last two stanzas, heightened into psychic drama and complexity by the logic of the poem's structure, as simple as it might seem. In the first stanza the speaker introduces "the man" through the descriptive details of his morning routine; then in the others he draws back from the intimacy of the setting he has labored to establish, with an air of detachment, beginning each stanza as he does with the synoptic "This is what the man is…" So there is the "before" and the after of this man's daily life. That he is not named is part of the ambiguity; despite the intimate moments we are privy to, he remains somehow distant, apart, his namelessness symbolic of that. The intimacy, in short, is an illusion, or at best a red herring. This complexity is testament to Smith's skill as a poetic strategist, and his language use, his carefully manipulated diction, to his equal skill as a tactician.

The apparent intimacy is established with the first word of the poem: "Curling." The man doesn't grip his coffee cup, he doesn't squeeze it; his fingers "curl" around it, fingers and cup mutually shaped, and he "cradles" it, watching the steam "rise," noting how each finger "shapes the fog of morning"—a lovely synesthetic image—leaving his "fingerprints upon the 'swirl' (quotes mine) of time." Around him he hears the "tick" of a clock, the birds in his garden just starting to "sing," a dog "startled" by the arrival of dawn, and the "thud" of the morning paper outside his door. All of these words soothe, easing us into a sense of tranquility, of peace—the garden the man mentions resonant with a hint of Eden. But, ambiguously, "startled" and "thud" jar just a bit, each a tonal note slightly off key, slightly dissonant, transitioning to and foreshadowing what occurs in the next two stanzas.

In stanza two, more turns than just the ignition in the family car. Immediately, parameters are established. What was almost Edenic begins to erode, and it does so with one vital word: "before." Eden was before, the Land of Nod, after. Eden, presented here as a domestic setting, either rural or suburban or both, and personified by "the man" himself, the speaker says is what the man's wife imagined before any thought of diamonds and "other souls, presumably marriage and children—you know, that old vision called the American Dream. Then the speaker spends the rest of the stanza riffing on the "little things" that shape a man: the "scent of his chemical balances," the "colors he sees/ as sun rises over the blasted buildings of his city," and the "tiniest bits of the universe," its atoms, that "pulled together" to make him "unique in all of time." Even though the speaker is describing the man in, literally, such glowing terms, the language is ambiguous: The man smells, the sunrise he admires is in a city of blasted buildings, and the building blocks of who he is are the tiniest in the universe. Here, too, the structure does its work superbly. Think Stephen Dedalus, in *A Portrait of the Artist as a Young Man*, when, starting from one finite point on the map, his village, he imagines a concentric expansion outward—county, country, continent, world, universe—himself reduced to an infinitesimal dot, an ultimate reduction of identity. Likewise, the man in "He Does What It Takes": his scented self, the blasted buildings, the city, and micro- or macro-cosmically, the universe.

Almost resignedly, "This is what he is," the speaker repeats at the beginning of stanza three, almost as if the repetition (each a clone of the other) will lend more credence to the man's uniqueness. But then comes another telling and vital word: "machine." What has been established up to this point about the man is his presumed uniqueness, mundane as it is. Notice, though, the speaker doesn't say *who* the man is, but *what* he is. That is a telling distinction. The man is unique even in his commonality. Ambiguity has morphed into paradox. Everyman is just that—every man. And yet not. If the man "goes out each morning" (a diurnal routine) to do the bidding of the machine, isn't he part of it? And what exactly is the machine? The man himself, his DNA an exact copy of that of all those other billions? The chemicals and atoms of which he is made? Or is the machine the world of commerce, the "hum" of which "fills his veins"? Perhaps it is all of these. One thing is certain—not only is the language and imagery and metaphor exact and perfectly attuned to the context of this poem, but the ambiguity inherent to its last line simply perfect and utterly unexpected. Exactly what love is it the man is whispering of "with each breath he takes"? Is it of his wife? Of his small piece of Eden? Of himself perhaps, his uniqueness? Or is it of the machine he serves—the business that is the business of America, that commerce moving like blood through his veins?

By now it's obvious that Jack responds to poems that are intelligently structured, deeply rooted in expressive and precise language; poems that aren't afraid of complexity, that don't back down from dissonance and darkness, hinted at or overt, yet are fearlessly lyrical, too. If "He Does What It Takes" veers toward darkness, toward shadows, and what light it casts is at best ambiguous, "Rivers Will Flow" is an outright celebration of light and all that it symbolizes. It is a poem that sings of rebirth and love, of the human and the natural, all in the context of a wholesome balance, not of opposites but of complementarities. Clearly, having chosen this poem, too, Jack the editor is open to a full-throated poetic rendition of an existence that is fueled by light, not dark.

Again, any rendering, whether of dark or light, begins with language. As with the first stanza of "He Does What It Takes," the diction lines up in the first stanza of "Rivers Will Flow," collectively establishing an atmosphere of serenity. Abundance and fecundity are its key notes: "So much snow," "bloom," "warmed," "melt," "green" (twice), "colors," "roots," "fill" and "waters." Despite an unseasonably heavy snow, spring is coming on, with all that it traditionally implies, and even under a "blanket of ice" (a paradoxical trope) life in all its glory is stirring and persevering, even the tulip and daffodil shoots, having lost "their green/ retain their green beneath the balance of all colors" (white the combining of all colors, thus a balance), their roots ultimately filling "with the water of time."

Structurally, that "time," the last word of the first stanza, does its work. Ironically, it connotes timelessness, which of course hearkens back to what the speaker has been describing—the timeless cycle of birth, death, rebirth—while simultaneously reminding the speaker that human time is brief, which he in turn reminds his lover of, his "lazy head." Such a transition that both reaches back and moves ahead is to be prized, as we can be sure Jack did. In stanza two, the speaker addresses his lover directly, an intimacy much more present in "Rivers Will Flow," in relational terms. The speaker from this point on is not just a troubadour of natural beauty, but the classic troubadour of love. Contrary to the man in "He Does What It Takes," the speaker here has no confusion as to who he is. In this brief lyric identity equals lover, of both nature and the human.

Significantly, too, "time" is repeated twice in stanza two, at the end of lines one and five, following its placement at the end of the last line of stanza one. Structurally again, this is repetition used smartly and tellingly for emphasis. The repetition channels Marvell's dictum that "Time's wingèd chariot [is] hurrying near," which is precisely what the speaker is reminding his lover of. The imagery that follows is simply lush and beautiful, enough so to attract even the most hard-bitten of editors, and certainly Jack: the abundance of snow that, melting, will make rivers "flow" like, it suggests, his seed; his lover's breasts "cherry trees in a ceramic urn," a lovely image charged with sexuality (and suggestive of art and human creativity, both procreative and aesthetic); his hands "remember[ing]" her breasts, his fingers "urg[ing] their nipples." Rather than this scene being "charged with the grandeur of God," it is charged with the grandeur of human sexuality, something that, if handled well, as here, is attractive on a deeply fundamental level to anyone, not just an editor.

Now the speaker doubles his attempt to rouse (pun intended) his lover by repeating not once but twice his clarion call, "Wake up, wake up," adding, "in your giving of life"—which, while hinting perhaps at pregnancy, rounds back to the natural fecundity described in stanza one—and "in your time/ where all the shadows have fallen into memory." Then the speaker ends with "Wake," which stands alone, a single word, the last of the poem, and a dramatic final flourish. There is nothing suggestive about it; it is an imperative, as if he is saying, after what he has pictured for her in such detail, she has no choice. The shadows are gone. There is only light.

So those are the poems that Jack took—one shimmering with light, the other tinged with darker shades—and this, my explication of why I think he did. Have I unearthed every reason he seized on them and not the others in Smith's submission? Probably not. But surely their lyric intimacy, their efficacy of structure, and their supple control of language are primary, as they should be. Beyond these and other technical considerations, there is that subjective, intuitive moment of recognition, that Aha! moment that an editor, like a poet, either has or doesn't and is not measurable, as it should not be. For better or worse, then, this is my dressing down of an editor, first name Jack—a dressing down in the good sense of stripping to the poetic bone each poem, both individually and in tandem, and excavating the aesthetic values he brought to bear in his decision to accept them.

Does Jack, or any editor, always get it right? Probably not—no more than anybody gets everything right in any area of artistic endeavor. That said, Jack's selection of Smith's two brief lyric poems reflects clearly his aesthetic predilections, his skill at separating out fully realized poems from the thousands that cross his desk, and his obvious devotion to the art he serves. As writers, our chore always is to come to terms with disappointment and trust the judgment of an experienced editor, remembering that rejection doesn't necessarily equate to a lack of merit; it often means simply that the editor can't use that particular poem or poems, for one of any number of reasons. As poet and editor John Amen writes in one of his poems, "I edit my masterpiece/ by morning I let it go." Exactly. An editor lets a poem go, and the poet must have the grace, and common sense, to let go of the editor's letting go. In other words, move on…

Good editors wear hats of many different shapes, sizes and colors: They're critics; they're advisors; they're fellow writers; they're literary allies; sometimes even friends, if mostly at a distance; they're fellow lovers and teachers of literature; and perhaps most important, they're avid and devoted readers. As a poet myself, I no doubt will again curse and flop about, caught on the hook of my despair and wounded ego, but soon enough I will thrash my way free and go about my usual writerly business, abetted by my own devotion to the art I love, by my own seemingly unending tenacity, and by an insistent editor with tenacity equal to mine and to the task at hand, arriving at a poem equal in quality to my particular talent. That is his service to the poem, and to me, the poet in his keeping. Jack, I hope I've demonstrated, is one of those editors, at one time or another donning each of those hats. Humility dictates we thank him for his devotion and tenacity, and to cite John Amen again, agree that we ought to "resist more/ & surrender quicker."

So thank you, Jared Smith, for your two poems so resonant with wonder; and thank you, Jack, for bringing to your task as editor an equally resonant sense of wonder.

*Permission granted by the author

Poet and editor, Jack Bedell

Crazy Dance: What Actually is Being Said in Father/Son Poems

Like too many sons, I didn't know my father well. He was a military man and he and my mother divorced when I was four. So we weren't in each other's life very much. I actually lived with him and my Japanese stepmother, Emiko, only twice—during my senior year of high school and, after a year back east, my freshman year of college, both of which were in Oregon where he was stationed for several years. After he retired they moved to Vacaville, California, where I visited several times over the years and last saw my father alive.

On one visit, my father and Emiko both loving to play the slots, we drove to Reno. Halfway there, at the very summit of the mountains, we pulled off to stretch our legs and to enjoy the panoramic view. Standing there side by side, neither my father nor I said a word for several minutes. Then, out of the California blue, my father said something that revealed much about him and over the years has allowed me to at least somewhat plumb his real emotional complexity, something he rarely displayed.

"You know," he said, staring straight ahead into immense mountain space, "It's bad enough you're going to die, but to know you are—that's hell. It's like carrying a rucksack stuffed with rocks all your life."

Talk about the knowledge of good and evil. Without consciously knowing it, my father had uttered a sentiment nearly biblical in its profundity. Despite his usual affected unconcern about death and our place in the world since the Fall, a stance you'd expect from a military man, with that statement my father had revealed a much deeper angst than I, as a typically self-obsessed young man in his thirties, had even begun to suspect. Plus, he had couched it in a metaphor that echoed the Sisyphus myth.

Which brings me to that poetic subset, father poems. At some point, just as with mother poems, every male poet has written one—or more likely, many. So many, whether lyric or narrative, have been written that some critics disdain them, assigning them to a necessary but regrettable juvenilia. And it's true: There are thousands of them, poems in every conceivable form and written from every possible emotional stance—anger, loss, grief, resentment, envy, even hatred, and most important, love, because with love comes redemption, whether the father's, the son's, or more likely, both.

Probably most poets have their favorite father poems, and I'm no different. One of my very favorites is Robert Hayden's little lyric, "Those Winter Sundays," which I love because, by the end, the speaker is both chained to incredible pain and unshackled by redemption—pain when he realizes the depth of his father's love and sacrifice, all those years of toil and doing without—and the ignorance displayed in his indifference as a child; redemption in the guilt-fueled love for his father he arrives at in adulthood. Too late, it seems, is not definitive; redemption means it is never too late.

Hayden's is one approach a father poem can take. Another is that of an amazing poem by Colorado poet, Jared Smith:

FATHER,
your grandson is struck sterile
among choices you have left behind.
The compass that carried you through Eagle Scouts is gone;
the badges worn across your chest, dust like the degree from Harvard.
I am a cold point beneath the winter sky,
a dust mote upon a string played obbligato between galaxies,
and soon enough there will be no mountain meadows
for your descendants to walk among.
Darkness burns away on the wings of a moth
flaring itself into a place you have come to know.
The maples I climbed on have gone,
with no more power in their roots to shade your window.
The driveway I carried your suitcase along that last day
has been blacktopped three times that I know
and the weeping cherry you never knew was planted
by my son whom you never knew

and dwarfs a house on the other side of town.
You knew the lady slippers and May apples,
showed me where tiger salamanders lay beneath logs,
called ground cover by all its varied names
spoke 16 languages and read from the books of the dead,
strode with an urgency through urban forests
and took the train to work each day. Tickets, getting
tickets please. Sandwiches in paper bags.
The aurora borealis blows through the cells of my bone,
igniting them so that they are torn apart and scattered in the solar wind.
What was it that you wanted to achieve. Why
did we wear our tight shirt collars to expensive hotels
or spend long years sweating our fears into foreign sheets.
I am older now than you were on that day
when you lay down in a blueberry patch and died
on vacation beneath a Minnesota sky.
After the stroke, we had three days before you rose,
and the light in your eyes seemed to go on forever without finding words.
In listening ever since among the stars, I have been paralyzed
and have raised flawed children who are as wise as you
with no desire to pass it on.

Smith's poem is darker, much darker. By the end the speaker hasn't so much laid claim to redemption as he has an utter honesty, and in that honesty a controlled complexity and something that passes for intimacy. All the usual themes are present and accounted for—isolation, loss, grief, issues of identity, death. Then there is what actually is being said, and this, as is not unusual with poetry, is conveyed through a progression of detail, through careful diction, metaphor, symbol, and most crucial to the poem, interconnecting layers of imagery: cosmic, which acts reductively; natural, gleaned from the father's instruction; domestic, presented in terms of both home and travel; and religious, conveyed through language and symbol.

"Father," is not a simple poem. How could it be? Father/ son relationships are never simple, just as all human relationships are not, no matter their surface appearance. To begin with, there is that title. It is significant that the father is addressed as Father, not Dad or Daddy or Pop or Papa. It lends an immediate formality of address, furthered by the comma. Grammatically, of course, the comma is correct, required after a name of address, and "Father" acts as a name. But a comma is a pause, too, and here it could imply a hesitation, even reluctance, thus a distancing. And no wonder, given what we learn in the course of the poem about this particular father/ son relationship. Revelation of any emotional sort should give us pause.

The poem is a dramatic monolog, and revelation, wanted and unwanted, is that genre's province. It is ironic, too, given the distancing that has been established from the get-go. Interestingly, the poem isn't structured as straightforward cause/ effect; rather, it is structured more along the lines of effect/ cause(s)/ effect. So even in logical terms it is a complex affair. Outright, we learn that "your grandson is struck sterile." Whoever or whatever the father was, his effect generationally is made abundantly clear with that one word, "sterile," perhaps the single most important in the poem because it encapsulates so much of what ultimately is revealed. Note that the poem ends by rounding back to this sterility: the speaker is "paralyzed," has raised "flawed children" who, even if they have inherited the wisdom of the father, have "no desire to pass it on." Generationally, the father's legacy is a dead end. Bleak indeed—but honest in its appraisal, and true to who and what the speaker thinks the father was and what he is actually saying about him.

Perhaps an equally important word is the one that follows "sterile": "choices," specifically, those emblems of choice the father "left behind"—a compass and Boy Scout badges gone to "dust like the degree from Harvard." So the father was an achiever, and as such looms large both as example for and goad to the speaker and his "flawed children." Achievement, we are told over and over again by our culture, is everything, that it gives meaning to a life; but it also can be a burden to those who come after, fomenting resentment, an abiding sense of failure, of never measuring up, rebellion, and in extreme cases, hatred.

Call these first details of the father's youthful life domestic imagery. Immediately following, there is a shift to the speaker, to the father's effect on him specifically:

I am a cold point beneath the winter sky,
a dust mote upon a string played obbligato between galaxies,
and soon enough there will be no mountain meadows
for your descendants to walk among.

Besides these lines being simply beautiful poetic expression, powerful language powerfully used, they abruptly widen Smith's imagistic reach from the domestic to the cosmic. Here's our little nowhere man sitting in a nowhere cosmos. The ecological catastrophe is not the father's fault, but metaphorically it again measures his effect on his immediate heirs, in a most devastating way.

Then comes another shift, into the natural, temporal world—natural imagery. If the cosmic imagery presents the speaker's sense of loss and isolation in large, the natural imagery brings us back down to earth, to the temporal, and through a progression of factual details, reveals more of who and what the father was. So the stone-cold darkness of the cosmos "burns away on the wings of a moth/ flaring itself into a place you have come to know."

Structurally, as well as imagistically, a transformation has occurred: from a dust mote "played obbligato between galaxies" in an icy void to a very earthly moth, darkness burning "away on <its> wings." Fire symbolically can be either creative or destructive, so at best this transformation is an ambiguous one. Partly this is because of what follows: a referencing of natural phenomena that reveal both the father's botanical expertise and again the speaker's acute sense of loss. Loss comes first—the maples he climbed as a boy are no more, "with no more power in their roots to shade" the father's window; the dirt and/ or gravel (natural) driveway the speaker carried the father's suitcase "along that last day/ has been blacktopped (unnatural) ; and the "weeping cherry you never knew was planted/ by my son whom you never knew," dwarfing "a house on the other side of town." All this natural imagery points to dislocation, separation, isolation and loss.

Next comes the upside of the father's knowledge of flora and fauna, which segues into other facts about the father, all of which further nothing for the speaker but that excruciating sense of isolation and loss. The father, we learn, taught his son to identify lady slippers, May apples, tiger salamanders where they "lay beneath logs" and the "varied names" of ground cover. Then in rapid succession we learn that the father "spoke 16 languages," "read from the book of the dead" (Tibetan, we assume), "strode with an urgency through urban forests," and rode the train to work: "Tickets, getting/ tickets please." Is it a coincidence that with this phrase Smith is channeling Eliot's barman ("HURRY UP PLEASE IT'S TIME") in *The Wasteland*?

This father was, then, intelligent, learned, strong and motivated (note the word "strode"). He was a naturalist, a linguist, a scholar and some sort of professional, we assume, a commuter who rode the train, itself a symbol of industry, of expansion, of might, into the city each day (like, perhaps, the mob crossing London Bridge?) and bestrode its "urban forests." He almost seems like a character stepping out of one of Ayn Rand's novels, at least to the diminished figure of the speaker. As Smith puts it,

> The *aurora borealis* blows through the cells of my bone,
> igniting them so that they are torn apart and scattered in the solar wind.

There's that surreal cosmic imagery again, beautifully and poetically phrased. And there's that fire imagery again; only this time there is nothing ambiguous about it. Clearly, it's destructive here—the *aurora borealis* as both beauty and beast. Clearly, too, this speaker is a son who is very much conflicted. By now, both figuratively and factually, a definitive picture of the reasons for this has begun to come into focus.

Evidently, we now learn, the father's occupation, whatever it was, had him traveling, and, not necessarily by choice, his family, too. The speaker testifies to their discomfort and even fear when he asks, rhetorically, "Why/ did we wear our tight shirt collars to expensive hotels/ or spend long years sweating our fears into foreign sheets." It's telling, and technically shrewd, that each direct question ends, not with a question mark, but a period. The speaker knows that his questions are rhetorical, of necessity; the father is, after all, dead. There can be no answer, not from the source anyway.

And so we come, both literally and figuratively, to the end of this complexly moving poem. We learn that the speaker is "older now" than the father was the day he "lay down in a blueberry patch and died"—a fitting merging of the father and the natural world he obviously esteemed—in Minnesota, of a stroke. Here we have a speaker who endures a conflicted heart, and a father who dies of a literally broken heart, an example of how Smith uses irony sparingly, but bitingly when he does.

Similarly, he uses symbol, as we have seen already, and does so masterfully to close out his poem. Earlier, when the speaker referred to that blacktopped driveway, he said it had been paved over three times that he knew of; now we learn that the father had lingered three days before he "rose/ and the light in <his> eyes seemed to go on forever without finding words," for which he, the speaker, has been "listening ever since among the stars," to no avail. It's clear what Smith intends. On the literal level, the speaker is referring to the father's stroke-induced muteness, how that made his lingering all the more terrible, intensifying his sense of separation, isolation, loss. Symbolically, though, through his use of religious imagery, it brings to the poem an aching, almost unendurable pathos. Implicitly compared to Christ, the father suffered for three days on the cross that is his stroke, then finally rose, ascending into some place other, beyond recall, beyond the speaker's agonizing desire for touch, for the connection that has always eluded him.

Father/ son poems are, always, about connection, or too frequently, a lack thereof. Certainly, this is true of Smith's poem, which lays out the consequences of disconnection in detailed and movingly poetic language. But what is it precisely that is being said? Perhaps another, much more directly located poem provides a succinct answer to that question: "Fathers and Sons," by Colorado poet laureate, David Mason.

Mason's poem focuses on one moment of interaction between a father and son. The son is attempting to help his incapacitated father unbuckle, pull his trousers down and sit on the toilet:

> How he had wiped my bottom
> half a century ago, and how
> I would repay the favor
> if he would only sit.

The father resists. "Somewhere," Mason writes, "a man of dignity would not be laughed at," and ends the poem:

> He could not see
> it was the crazy dance
> that made me laugh,
> trying to make him sit
> when he wanted to stand.

And there it is, what Smith actually is saying in his riveting poem: that a father/ son relationship, specifically his and his father's, is inevitably a conundrum. How do you connect with a father who on so many levels can only disconnect? How do two individuals who are both alike and not alike locate themselves on common ground? Like Mason's son, how can the son in Smith's poem make his father heed his importuning? Make him respond to love with love—an active, open expression, or at least a forthright recognition, of love?

Perhaps what Smith and Mason are saying is that there is no one answer to such a human conundrum, that indeed all there is, is the crazy dance. One thing is certain: Despite any critical dismissiveness, father/son poems will continue to be written, which in itself is an act of love, no matter the thicket of emotions and actions or inactions and the resultant and various conflicts. Redemption can be obtained in large ways, but more often in small, unanticipated ways.

After my father died, I traveled to Vacaville to attend to his burial (cremation) and personal affairs, and to provide Emiko the strong support she needed. My father had died unexpectedly, in hospital, probably from some drug or anesthesia he was allergic to. He never woke after what was supposed to be routine minor surgery, went into a coma, and died. As far as I knew he never was aware of what was happening, never suffered. I was grateful for that, which, combined with the focus my duties required, left me no time to ponder the immensity of our loss, let alone grieve.

Then, a few days after the funeral and burial of his ashes, I was combing through his belongings and in his and Emiko's bedroom closet, tucked in the back corner of a high shelf, I stumbled on something that released both my tamped-down grief and great joy and love simultaneously.

Over the years, besides my one published collection of poetry at the time and a couple of anthologies containing poems of mine, I had sent my father copies of various journals in which my work had appeared. I always assumed he wouldn't read them, or really place too much value on them. He *was* a military man, and I never saw him read much of anything other than newspapers. How wrong I was. When I pulled them from the shelf, I saw they were stacked neatly, arranged chronologically in the order of their reception, and wrapped with pink ribbon, tied into a big bow.

Right then, at that precise moment in mid-May, 1989, I learned that my father, despite the separation and lack of much real connection in our lives, actually had loved me. And I learned how much loss I was confronting, and how much love I'd lost and how much I'd gained. Tears and smiles born of joy—that's the conundrum. Absence was what the future held from that day onward; yet within it, blossoming like a night flower in its blackness, was that stack of journals wrapped with its pink ribbon and bow. I had never felt such aching loss and such great redemptive love.

This paradox is, in both Smith's and Mason's poems, and in Hayden's too, what defines their particular father/ son relationships. And it defines my father's and mine. Language, no matter how poetic, cannot replace what is lost, what is grieved, resented, loved, feared, hated; but it is what we have. And in the hands of these superb poets, it's a gift. As such, it is necessary. Both the act of poetic writing and the resultant poem itself is beautiful and redemptive. This, too, is what actually is being said. It is the special province of father/ son poems—and yes, of mother/ daughter poems, too.

Theodore Roethke, in his rightly famous poem, "My Papa's Waltz," writes that, for the little boy hanging onto his drunken father, "Such waltzing was not easy." The crazy dance never is. And to capture it in the stirring, beautifully rendered language of poetry is equally as difficult. The poets discussed here have. We are richer for it.

Poet Jared Smith

Random Wizards

I Beg You, Ezra

> *gloss your text.*
> *You've left me desolate and vexed.*
>
> —Johnny Wink

Every English teacher I ever had talked about levels of meaning, particularly when it came to poems, especially those of such inscrutables as Pound and Eliot and Stevens. That a poem has multiple meanings was a cardinal rule. Such possibilities are what make poetry "difficult." As a student falling in love with poetry, I accepted this both as cause and effect. But questions arise, two especially: What exactly is meant by levels of meaning? How are those levels achieved?

Diction is the first, and most obvious, way. Word connotation is not exactly rocket science, difficult and complex though it might be in context. Words can mean more than one thing, and sometimes those meanings can seem contradictory. Nothing new there.

Obviously, too, syntax—the construction of sentences—can complicate meaning, not to mention the music, the linguistic and voice tonality of the poem, its rhythms, able to both open up and conceal meaning. Nothing new there, either.

Imagery, individual and patterned, also can contribute to levels of meaning, as can metaphor and symbol. By their very nature, images can suggest without being explicit, in that one has to "read" the image, to interpret it. A flower is only a flower, or is it? Different flowers can mean different things: A daffodil is not a rose, a rose is not a begonia. Red roses aren't white roses, either. Literary and cultural traditions can add another interpretive complexity to meaning. In these cases, images become something more—symbols. Think Wars of the Roses! Metaphors, too—by their very nature, complexity of meaning is unavoidable. They are, after all, in the business of directly comparing two unlike things. How can they not be complex? Again, though, nothing new there.

So. Language itself, syntax, imagery, metaphor and symbol: All contribute to and make inevitable multiple meanings in a poem. But is that all? Levels of meaning, as a concept and application, must itself mean more than grammar and literary techniques. There must be something more structured, more profound, mustn't there?

Well, yes. Certainly structure itself can contribute. Think, for example, of the villanelle. All those repetitions, at once the same and slightly varied, result in not only a beautiful music but in a beautiful complexity of meaning, too. But that's only part of the story. Poems that incorporate both lyric and narrative elements, not to mention simultaneous thematic concerns and what we might call multiple "worlds," are poems with deeply textured and even seemingly contradictory intentions. To say they're complex is understatement of the first order.

Now let's actually look at a poem—this one, from the collection Seven Ways to Prune a Grapefruit, by Arkansas poet Johnny Wink, titled "Slow, However, His Marches Be":

There at the poetry reading, about to read
A poem about The White Rabbit, I asked my small
Audience how many of them had known The White
Rabbit and only several had, a fact that made me
Strangely sad. I say "strangely" because, Time
Gets bent on marching on. The White Rabbit went
Down in the raw, dark, drizzly heart of November
Seven years ago, and, for God's sake, this is
A college, and it's all about marching them through—
Students coming and going and going and coming, trickling
In and out of your life the way leave-takers make for
The busy door of this reading. Of course only
A handful knew The White Rabbit! Get a grip.
I'll get a grip alright. Next year, I" troy out for
The marching band. I'll get Ouida Keck to give
Me tuba lessons. I'll play tuba in the band.
I'll get a grip. On that tuba so when Time,
Famous for marching on, goes marching on by

The marching band, I'll clout the bastard with
The well-gripped tuba Ouida Keck will have
Taught me to play. And, as Time lies there,
Cindery on the field, I'll say, "What *then*, bitch?"
Unless my guess is wrong, though, Time will get back up,
Maybe laughing, and doubtlessly go marching on.

The first thing one notices about this poem is its down-to-earth, direct, colloquial language and, thus, its speaking voice. At first glance, it doesn't seem particularly complex, let alone its meaning having levels. It comes off as an intimate self-exhortation: the phrase "get a grip," so colloquial it's clichéd, occurring no less than three times. This is deceptive.

The second thing one notices is the wry humor it displays. Subtle in the first stanza, it surfaces fully in the second. The whole notion of "getting a grip" by learning to play—of all instruments!—a tuba in a marching band is really very funny, its over-the-top humor serving to set off and emphasize the actual serious issues the speaker is confronting: the apparent death of someone—probably a fellow teacher nicknamed The White Rabbit, itself funny—; the relentless march of Time (which outmarches even the marching band); mortality—The White Rabbit's, the speaker's own and by extension all of ours, and its corollary, the slow erosion of our selves in memory.

So, in this poem, complexity of meaning resides in the deceptively everyday language, in the smokescreen of a self-deprecating humor and in the imagery. But even more, the levels of meaning inherent to the poem are embedded in the narrative elements, in the multiple thematic concerns, and in the "worlds" it incorporates. There are several: that of the fairy tale (in this case, *Alice in Wonderland*), poetry readings, music (marching bands), academia, and science—physics (the nature of time, implied black hole).

How's that for a complex web of realities? Add to these the ironic title—Whose marches are slow? The speaker's? The dead White Rabbit's? Contradictorily, Time's?—and Wink's poem exemplifies those levels of meaning English teachers like to go on about. That the speaker's wry humor is both a coping mechanism and an ironic way of emphasizing the seriousness of the poem's central thematic concerns is on display from the beginning.

Like The White Rabbit, poetry is elusive—so much so that the audience is "small" and "leave-takers make for/ The busy door of this reading." Talk about connotation! Consider how much that one word, "busy," conveys. We laugh at such oblique tips of the hat to reality, but we also know it often is a painful one. To make matters worse, few of the audience "had known The White/ Rabbit," which makes the speaker sad—"strangely so," given the bending of Time as it marches on. (That "Gets bent" is also a pejorative colloquial expression should not be lost on us; certainly it isn't on the poet.) That he is referring to the one who had died ("went/ Down"—our black hole) seven years earlier is obvious. But what if he also is referring to The White Rabbit of Wonderland? What if few in the audience had even read it? Again, complexity. Levels of meaning.

Then there is a turn. The speaker upbraids himself for any false expectations he might have had of his audience, which is of course comprised of students. Analogous to those leaving the reading, they come and go, "trickling/ In and out of your life…" Why should he think they would have known The White Rabbit, dead already for seven years? "Get a grip," he commands himself, and beautifully opens the second stanza with "I'll get a grip alright." Besides the obvious emphasis and transition the repetition provides, it also leaves us suspecting that in fact he won't. Not really.

Accordingly, stanza two, while more overtly humorous, is also edgy. The very absurdity of getting a grip by playing a tuba in that marching band, not to mention the offbeat name, Ouida Keck, contributes a certain shrillness in tone, which the language picks up on: "I'll clout the bastard," "What *then*, bitch?" Funny, yes. But even more, the humor and the edginess make manifest the speaker's own deep sorrows—for the loss of a colleague and probable friend; for the gulf in time between his memories and the total unknowingness of the students; for the plight of poetry; for the albatross of mortality; and for the unstoppable march of time:

> Unless my guess is wrong, though, Time will get back up,
> Maybe laughing, and doubtlessly go marching on.

And so will we. Those last two lines are an apt description of the poem itself. "Doubtlessly," both in the sense of implacability and without doubt, not only will Time rise, dust itself off and, laughing, move on, but so will we, the readers, after finishing "Slow, However, His Marches Be." And so, too, the poet silently hopes, will his poem. What makes this poem so memorable is its gutsiness in approach and subject, its grace under pressure, and its honesty—all three of which demand a certain complexity of meaning, of levels of emotion and thought. Despite the hint of false bravado in the face of loss, mortality and unstoppable Time, we come away somehow uplifted, if not by the truth of those enormities, then by the very human balancing of their contradictory effects in the poem, and by extension in all our lives. We weep, but we also endure. And we celebrate our human capacity to endure. Such are the polarities of a complex life, and of complex poems.

Such poems are like layered birthday cakes. Each layer can be coated differently. One might be lathered in strawberry jam, one in whipped cream, another in raspberry. Each layer thus will have its own unique taste, but they all will merge in a collective taste, too. So it is with levels of meaning in a poem—certainly in Johnny Wink's wonderful poem. And, too, besides the separate tasty layers of the cake, there is the cake itself, that baked solidity. Likewise, in the end, there is the language and the definitive structure of the poem. That equally wrought solidity. That artful enterprise.

While poems might at times leave us feeling desolate and abandoned on the rocky shore of the opaque, they more often are like wild tangles of driftwood left behind by the tides—raw material ready for sifting and shaping (much like the ingredients of those birthday cakes). Like Pound and Eliot and Stevens, who so often succeeded in shaping poems into an accessible, shimmering art, surely Johnny Wink has shaped this poem with intelligence, insight, skill and honesty into something with textured levels of meaning. Finishing it, one can only say, Please, I beg you, Johnny, more, more…

In the Kingdom of Babies: Galway Kinnell

To say I like all of Galway Kinnell's poems would be, at best, a childish courtesy, and, at worst, a caramel-appled lie. So I won't. To like all of anything another man might say is fantasy, implying as it would perfection of a higher order than is possible—or even wise. And Galway Kinnell's is far too major a talent to allow of such simplicity. Rather, his demands a willingness to skirmish—not with squads of telling similes, which he dislikes, preferring more the thrill of head-on verb collisions, but with flower petals of the consciousness dislodging pavements and the ragamuffin surfaces and superstructures of the contemporary world and thrusting sexually into the primal darkness that is subterranean as city sewage ways; into, that is, the love-damp kingdom of the babies seconds after their ejection into blue-faced breath. Such is the menace and glory of Kinnell's work, the talon and the wing. Such is what his poems presume, and such is what his poems deliver. As he cites his mentor, Rilke, as a preface to his *Book of Nightmares*:

> But this, though: death,
> the whole of death,—even before life's begun,
> to hold it all so gently, and be good:
> this is beyond description!

Galway Kinnell knows that the nightmare is the dream reversed, defining itself like the double face of Janus, Roman god of gates; knows, too, through the murk of darkness light reveals itself: the double dream of poets, Fools and gifted men; knows death and life are wedded, as the dream is to the dreamer; knows the Zero always hungers for the One.

So, no, I won't say I like all of Kinnell's poems. For if I did like all I should be keenly disappointed. What we want, and what his poems are, is poetry that is essential, not just likable; poetry that scratches on the tablets of the consciousness. What we want of all our major poets isn't maudlin music tailored to the hollow sound of clapping, not today when the mundane has been exalted into regions even dreams won't trek; what we want is the intestines, blood and gore and all, ripped out of the black gut of our humanity and hung like Kinnell's hen flowers from the fist of our dilemma. What we want, in short, is affirmation wrenched from the clandestine by the ragged crow-caw of our birthing, death-daring bell clapper of an existence. In the carnival we call the universe death sets the rules. But only life can play the game. And only life can win the prize.

Says Jamshid, the protagonist of Galway Kinnell's novel, *Black Light*: "That...is the way with poetry. When it is incomprehensible it strikes you as profound, and when you do understand it, it lacks common sense." Of Kinnell's poetry, however, we can say it is, without the sacrifice of common sense, indeed profound, and comprehensibly as glittering as stars above the vast Iranian desert across which Jamshid winds his way—into the drifting sand that is the Self.

Galway Kinnell has been affirming both the game and the prize—and winning.

The Name is Kumin, Not Frost

In *The Voice That is Great Within Us* the late Hayden Carruth says of Robert Frost that he is "a figure with whom younger poets, even the most rebellious, must come to terms." Maxine Kumin, in *Up Country: Poems of New England*, has done more than that: She has moved in on the Old Man's terrain; has staked her womanly claims and rewritten the script using the same materials.

Kumin's New England is rustic, inviting, consoling—on the surface. Beneath the outward calm there is the constant, sometimes violent, motion of unseen but felt currents of change. It has, like Frost's, its Quasimodos: the hermit carving his name so "someone after will take stock of him," and Henry Manley, Kumin's neighbor, "with a washpot warming on his woodstove"; it has its dwellings: old country houses, barns, graveyards; has its creatures: woodchucks, cows, horses, aquatic life, insects; it has its deaths: of people and creatures—which is exactly where the similarities end and Maxine Kumin's uniqueness begins.

Death, decay, destruction: All are omnipresent in *Up Country*. And that is as it should be. Any person with Kumin's obvious powers of observation is aware of such phenomena, even in their most minute forms. But what really wrenches, what really reflects her departure from the pastoral world of Frost is the *kinds* of death that occur. They are agonizingly contemporary: the desertion by time and people of the hamlet Poverty Corners, the woodchucks "gassed underground the quiet Nazi way," the dog "who lived a fool to please his king," the brood mare who lay down and died "full of false pride," the dreams of "all my dears/ picked famine dry," the "burned babies screaming," the country houses besieged by

> those hardy moderns who came in
> with their plastic cups and spoons
> and restorative kits
> for stripping the woodwork,
> torn between making over
> and making do.

The deaths Robert Frost wrote of (which so terrified Lionel Trilling) were those of the spirit, killed by cruel people and cruel landscapes. The deaths Maxine Kumin writes of are those of culture, values, concerns. She, like Frost, disarms with the simple beauty and peace of country things; then takes us, "oily and nude/ through mist, in chilly solitude," to the bottom of the pond, into the shadows of depth, where

> the packed hears of peepers are beating
> barely, barely repeating
> themselves enough to hang on.

What saves *Up Country* from pretentious, maudlin current pessimism is its ultimate affirmation that comes, paradoxically, in the midst of the terror and recognition:

> I am tired of this history of loss:
> What drum can I beat to reach you?
> To be reasonable
> is to put out the light.
> To be reasonable is to let go.

The fourth line evokes memories of Frost's "Once by the Pacific." But there is a difference: Whereas Frost's use of "put out the light" hinted at a prophetic inevitability, its use here is a spirited rejection of the prophecy. She will not be reasonable. She will not let go. That is the tender strength that underscores every poem, no matter how dark, how fearful. Yet the affirmation is not an easy one:

>   Even knowing
> that none of us can catch up with himself
>
> we are making a run
> for it. Love, we are making a run.

This also is as it should be. Kumin has the courage to strike out on her own "Cross Country by County Map," always secure, but *not* euphoric, in the knowledge that her "indoor people/ are waiting with bread and beer." The poems avoid maudlin optimism.

There is one other major difference between the New England of Kumin and that of Frost. It is obvious: Hers is a woman's, his, a man's. But what a difference. It has been pointed out by many critics that Frost understood Woman in some deep seated, intuitive way. Perhaps so. But how much more stunning it is when we encounter a woman who can understand and celebrate her own mystery, who can sing,

> I was the well
> that fed the lake that met my sea
> in which I sang *Abide with Me*.

And how refreshing it is, in this Age of Axes to Grind, when we encounter a woman who has achieved Liberation, who doesn't confuse femininity with simple self-indulgence, who doesn't confuse honest emotion with ennui, who doesn't confuse courtesy with chauvinism. And this is the ultimate triumph of *Up Country*: Every line, every poem is but a single note of the composition that is the unique totality of a human being, a Woman, named Maxine Kumin.

And the name *is* Kumin, not Frost.

The Gods, the Genes and a Fire Raging in the Belly

Williams Carlos Williams is a great poet. William Carlos Williams is not a great poet. Take your pick.

What I say is that William Carlos Williams is a very important *American* poet. Innovation and influence aside, Williams is "great" in the sense that his work is an embodiment of a particular inclination that is most peculiarly and historically American. "No ideas but in things," he said. Exactly. And his poems are, in their concretion, things, not ideas. In a most unique way the *what* of Williams' poems doesn't matter. It's his acute attention to the details of a landscape, inner or outer, that counts.

Philosopher, Williams is not. Great swooping rhetorician he's not. A doctor he was, and on life and death he cast his cold-eyed microscope. Even when he is dealing with the more-than-physical in life, say the aesthetic, Williams, like the tallest tree pushing ever higher toward the heavens with each passing year, keeps snug his roots in the great compost heap that is the earth. Williams is the best advertisement I know of for the stuff of which a poem is made. The caption, in small letters naturally, reads: *keep it real.*

To this one might well add: and keep *him* real. Young poets, just emerging from the shed skin of their adolescence, tend toward adulation. Williams, more than most poets, traditionally seems to be, at that early stage in poets' lives, the icon around which they rally—vociferously, and with little tolerance for any but an unquestioning belief that might have lifted Williams' eyebrows, if not his hair.

My neck hair rises even today when I think about J.E., my undergraduate bosom-buddy poet, with whom I sparred over Williams and his poetry for the entire four years, ending only with our BA's and my subsequent banishment to a graduate school in Washington State. To J.E., Williams was pure gold. To me, he was pyrite, Robert Frost being the only precious metal worthy of excavation. Now it's fifty-three years later, J.E. a distant memory, and I'm still citing Frost chapter and verse and getting away with it. The difference is that Frost is no longer the only poet I cite, and Williams, though he still isn't pure gold, *is* gold.

Once, in a local newspaper, there appeared a picture of the county sheriff on horseback, all decked out in what looked to be formal 19th-century riding garb: top hat and tails, cravat, white gloves. At first glance everything seemed right. The sheriff sat on his horse, the reins gripped properly in his right hand, his eyes locked in a squint against the sun, mouth slightly open. The horse, a roan, was all attention—nostrils flared, ears pointed forward, head and tail held high. "Sheriff Mounted on Horse" one might have titled a poem. But look again: The sheriff is leaning too far forward; his left hand is glued to the front edge of the English saddle; the horse's head and tail are high not because of strict attention but because the sheriff is reining him like that; the sheriff's feet are pointed down and out, not up as they would be if his weight were on the balls of his feet and he were sitting his horse properly.

No ideas but in things. Details. The brick and mortar of the poet. This, it seems to me, is the one lesson our young emerging poets can, and must, be taught—by example and in practice. Details. They make a difference. The details are the thing. Alter the thing and you alter the idea. This axiom applies to both the *what* of the poem and the *how*.

"Sheriff Mounted by his Horse" our poem might better be titled. And it most likely would by the better (and more playful) poet. And the better poet ought properly to be the end result of all our mentoring. Poets can't be made, but they can be taught the proper way to sit a horse. The rest is up to the gods, the genes and a fire raging in the belly. Williams would, I'm sure, agree.

J.E., I'm also sure, would still be unrepentant. Williams is, for him, as Williams was. He'd get no argument from me. The metal is now agreed upon, and even gold can differ in degree. Williams is not, for me, a Whitman. He is, however, the poet who most embodies the importance of those lengthy catalogs in Whitman's poems: *no ideas but in things*. Even when the things are so plentiful and the idea so grand.

Wizard

Sometimes That a Poem Is Masterful Is Enough

Reviews are of books, right? Generally, yes. And critical essays, or entire books of criticism, are about a writer's opus, and not coincidentally, its position in the canon, right? Again, yes. Sometimes, however, that a single poem is masterful enough to merit serious analysis is enough. Such is the case here. I have no large thematic or contextual point I wish to make. I simply find Jack Butler an admirable and masterful poet, and his poem, "Sundays in the Cemetery of Lost Childhood" a masterful poem: *

  the tall couples come, graceful and serious
but not too somber, and lay at the weathered granite
such particolored tribute as they can think of—
doll's mirrors, batteries, loose change, the lace
from ballet dresses, glass aggies. They choose, each,
the stones with their own names, although she may
drop a used lipstick, fire-engine red,
into that slight depression earth settles to,
never quite all heaped back, his plot, and he
may tether helium to a budding twig,
the young elm struggling from a mossy fault
in her rectangular casement. The favor, silver,
beats brightly in the little breeze, a heart
of lighter air.
  They are, improbably,
their own kind parents, and now may stroll or sit
in easy silence, hats off, coats over arms.

For all its hallowed and dappled slant, the light
leans less to prayer than relaxation, playing
in ripples across the river-gravel walks.

The birds are wasting time from branch to branch,
making it whistle as it disappears.
And something in all of this is like acceptance,
and something in all of this is like well-being.

Soon enough, the sun shifts, presses against them.
He loosens the car-key on its chiming ring.

They nod to others coming in the gate.
A slight sweat prickles at his hairline, on
her delicate upper lip.
    Her door, swung open,
releases volumes, the fragrance of heated leather.

He starts the motor, engineers a burst
of colder air. The locks snick shut in concert,
and they back out, devolve in stately S-curves
upon the access bridge, the stony creek
beyond whose fixed and glittering accident
they see their bypass arcing:
    A quick impression
of warehouse tenements, of railroad tracks
like stitches over the Frankenstein monster's brow,
and farther, a blur of tidy flower-beds,
frame houses, cyclone fences.
    Assume they exit
to winding boulevards, a thoroughfare
which rises to address great oaks, grand pillars.
Call it home. In a southern room, all glass,
someone has imagined sunlight falling across
red gladiolas on a wooden table.

They think of the other possibilities,
those rooms that may be out there somewhere
and therefore are: in which a man says, *Here,
come here—I promise it won't hurt*; in which

a woman pushing a market basket backslaps
a mouth to crooked silence; in which, cross-legged,
a child watches, as we might watch a face,
the window's image brighten on a plaster wall,
that water-stained silk of rainy after-light.

These things happen, are happening now, and worse.

Certainly there are hopeful agencies,
and decency occurs. They're here by grace,
but grace is a matter of chance, statistical.
Whiskey from crystal, then, lifted as if
it held, distilled, the best that one might hope for,
not health, but clarity and anodyne.

Later, they tuck themselves in. *Sleep tight*, they whisper,
and settle to those careful dreams in which
they never, not ever any more, ringside
at circuses, go naked, terrified
before that treacherous clown, their own happiness.

Only one question is pertinent, and the only one I am addressing: Why? Why do I find the poem masterful? Certainly it's not the theme, the loss of childhood and all it suggests, a theme poets before the Romantics and since have explored, and doubtless always will. Rather, it's the technical aspects of the poem and its structure.

First and foremost, it's Butler's always specific and often highly suggestive language—his diction—that alerts a reader to his technical prowess. If the diction is abstract it is made specific by context. When Butler writes, not far from the opening of the poem,

And something in all of this is like acceptance.
and something in all of this is like well-being,

the abstract "acceptance" and "well-being" become concrete because of the contextual concreteness of what comes after—for example, the sense of pain and violence and isolation in the long verse section near the end of the poem beginning, "They think of other possibilities." Butler is talking about much more than "birds wasting time." Equally impressive is the way word connotation both makes meaning more complex and makes clear what it means. In the long opening section the speaker asserts that the couples coming into the cemetery are "graceful and serious/ but not too somber...." Really? Why not somber? After all, they are in a cemetery, a place that makes many people somber, to say the least. Then he mentions "weathered granite" and the "slight depression earth settles to...." The language itself tells us why: The buried are not those who have died recently. Time has passed, enough so that the couples are there to offer "tribute," not mourn. Later the speaker says of the couple he seems to have settled on for the remainder of the poem that they are "their own parents," suggesting they have come to visit their real parents' graves.

So Butler's highly-charged diction marks this poem as truly masterful—a skill that is reflected throughout. Another, not so obvious, marker is the prosody. Butler is, technically, a master of traditional metrical verse, something rare in these post- and post-post-modern times. Yet it's not his use of meter that marks the poem; it's the masking of it. To a casual reader, the poem, with its broken lines and variable sectioning, appears to be free verse. But it isn't. Actually, the poem consists of five-beat, or pentameter, lines loosened considerably by extra syllables and metrical variations—spondees, anapests, trochees and so on. This is done with such felicity that unless he looks closely, or analytically, a reader won't notice. In effect, the poem comes off as conversational, even discursive at times, and yet invisibly tightly controlled. In short, Butler is a practitioner of the metrical mask.

Then there is structure. What is so masterful is the way Butler narrows, then widens, then narrows the locus of the poem. It opens with the action, such as it is, located in the cemetery where the "light/ leans less to prayer than relaxation" and the birds are making time "whistle as it disappears." Everything is contained by nature, "acceptance" and "well-being" a momentary lull, Frost's "stay against confusion." Soon, though, the sun "shifts, presses against them," and it's time to go, to leave tranquility behind, the sweat prickling the man's hairline and the woman's "delicate upper lip" emphasizing their fragility. Now the locus begins to widen, with the couple in their car; he starts the engine, the door locks "snick" shut and they "devolve in stately S-curves," the diction—"snick" suggesting snicker, "devolve" an unraveling—perfectly connotative of the change that is imminent: a further widening, both of physical location and sensibility.

The couple drives off and the cemetery gives way to an urban blight of "warehouse tenements" and "railroad tracks like stitches," suggesting a wounded, unnatural landscape, even a horrific one, the stitches "over the Frankenstein monster's brow." This in turn gives way to a suburban-like "blur of tidy flower-beds,/ frame houses, cyclone fences." Contrast this middle-class illusion of stability and security to the always regenerative natural world and the infinite absolute of death embodied by a cemetery—not to mention the loss of childhood, its innocence and imagination. Finally, after the couple exits to their world of boulevards, thoroughfares, "great oaks" and "grand pillars"—suggesting an exclusive neighborhood—their journey ends. Here the poem narrows again, to a simple southern room, possibly real, possibly not, defined by "sunlight falling across/ red gladiolas on a wooden table" that "someone has imagined." Perhaps the couple, perhaps not. Realities are beginning to blur, to dissipate like childhood itself. And with that dissipation comes a darkening—that section earlier alluded to of violence and isolation.

Butler's masterful use of structure leads to its perfect culmination at the end of the poem. Referring to the darkness of that last long section, the speaker concludes, "These things happen, are happening now, and worse." Ominous, that "worse," and though he immediately qualifies it with "hopeful agencies" and "decency," he in turn qualifies those: "They're here by grace," he says," but "grace is a matter of chance, statistical." Even grace is subject to a fundamental law of quantum mechanics. Whiskey in a crystal glass is the "best that one might hope for,/ not health, but clarity and anodyne." Ironically, the poem ends with the couple whispering *Sleep tight*, then settling into "careful dreams," connoting wariness, even fear. Dreams can be as dangerous as real experience. This being so, they will never allow themselves when "ringside at circuses" to "go naked, terrified/ before that treacherous clown, their own happiness." With this metaphor, Butler has conjured the perfect ending.

Children of course love circuses and clowns, and are open, nakedly so, and happy. But Butler's circus is the circus of life, and clowns are dangerous. They wear masks, too, are hidden behind paint and costumes. If happiness is a clown, then it is the most dangerous of all. Happiness can lead to vulnerability. In a sense, despite the shift in locale we end back where we started, in that cemetery of lost childhood. Essentially, that is, the structure of the poem consists of movement enclosed by stasis, the temporal by the infinite.

Right now, Jack Butler and his work are not much on the literary world's radar. But they should be. Probably more noted for his novels of a few decades ago, one of which was nominated for the Pulitzer and was on the *New York Times* best seller list, Butler's poetry is just as, or even more, I'd argue, natural to him. He is in his bones a poet. There are just as many poems as masterful as "Sundays in the Cemetery of Lost Childhood," each in its own unique way a text book example of the same technical and structural acumen. Context and canon aside, each of his powerful poems affirms that sometimes that a poem is masterful is indeed enough.

Certainly, this one does.

*Appeared in the Southwest Review *Permission to reprint granted by author*

Fixing the Shimmer: The Hard Art of Poetry

> *Sick of those who come with words, words but no language,*
> *I make my way to the snow-covered island.*
> —Tomas Tranströmer

Poetry is hard. How many times has any poet heard that? No, we usually respond, it isn't; you just have no experience with it. Well, yes. And no. Let's be honest: If hard means a total commitment to the experience of poetry, then yes, poetry *is* hard. But beyond this generality, what is it specifically that makes it hard? What is it that is unique to poetry that results in frustration and sometimes outright hostility?

Let's try to answer these questions by looking at one poem—Jack Butler's "On the Island,"* which alone illustrates why I hold him in such high esteem, and also demonstrates the difficulty of much of poetry generally:

ON THE ISLAND

I

We have spent all day at the beach
and I have wanted to say,
watching you sort patiently
the tossed cemeteries of shells
(each fanned-out print where a wave was
a complex field
of monument and skeleton in one
manifold character,
ready to shatter and rearrange, in a new wash,
its orders of burial, revelation)
how I love your ways: until, suddenly
with what has compelled you,

you come back to me grey-eyed,
in a low mood.

II

The waves begin at sea, but how?
Oh, we know how a sunk moon
drains at the gut of the water in that reiterated argument
a wide wind makes with tide and the broad currents,
and can suppose
the blow catches a flaw and flags it bigger—
but there in that first break, smaller than kisses,
that first snag from smoothness,
who can say why?

This the mathematicians call catastrophe,
speaking of fractals,
but I am not there in the clear center of their thought
to know what they mean,
and I am not out in the heart of the sea
where these processions augment, relent,
deliver themselves.

III

I am a man treading a thin shore,
who must report the hushed concussion of a million tongues
in the fuzzy rush of a single phrase,
who has seen the slap and glassy relapse
slipping back under
the thundering foot of the loud suck, but who
cannot remember a single event.

There was a silver-green that ran
the brassy tube of a rolling sunset
I memorized repeatedly like a man
staring into the bright of the fire

hoping to see headlines
announcing themselves from nowhere like angels of love,
but that green was always gone
on the whirling skin of my desire to see it,
although I spoke to you
insistently to help me miss it,
as if that was what we were for,
in double absence to fix the shimmer.

I could now enunciate
the hundreds of gulls and pelican, the heron, except that I hear

how anything I say
wheels away like a cry
into the violent, empty sky.

IV

You said my name, I am sure,
as I said yours over and over,
all carelessly,
a tag or a sort of adverb
expressing the vectors of hope, surprise, attention.

What goes on in the sun?
We came back burned to new awareness,
not fitting our skins exactly,
but still no wiser.

We came back to whiskey in glasses, to bad reception.
In the snows and sizzle of misspent photons,
we found ourselves performing a swollen service
that had its rising
millions of years before Proconsul
uttered a sound that might have been like
the word we agreed on, letting go: Good.

V

And now, since I cannot sleep,
and this is no thing we can say together,
let me appear to go down
to the astounding moon
dropping her actual slices
across the black glitter, impossible liquids.

It must seem to me now,
thinking the satisfaction of cold wet grit
under my foot,
the salt shock of a hollow air all bite and moisture,
harsh gift of volume to grateful lungs,
that I have not been, or noticed,
or represented or fully enjoyed a single pure thing
such as the greenest look
you have when you think I have made you happy,
a look that should consume
even the question
of why we come to the sea to be puzzled.

And so I will walk,
determined to see
at least one surge all the way through
with a simple spirit,
maybe that one, that one, or
that one there, antepenultimate, the third.

There are many reasons a poem can be difficult for even a seasoned reader, but in the case of "On the Island" there are these in particular: Butler's absolutely sophisticated mastery of craft; his penchant for startlingly unexpected imagery and metaphor; and his sure sense of sound—the musicality of language, rhythm, assonance, dissonance, and so on. What this one poem illustrates, then, is what we must call the necessary difficulty of any deeply imagined and realized poem, one that engages the inner human and outer natural worlds on multiple levels. This alone is enough to send a reader used to the more narrative lockstep of prose running for his aesthetic life.

Right away the visual appearance of the poem, its structural architecture, telegraphs its complexity. Since it is a sea poem one intention of the variously indented lines is obvious: to mirror the ebb and flow of tides. Less obvious is that they also mirror the ebb and flow of the speaker's thoughts: his conviction, his indecision; his assertions, his questions. And of course the metrical variations of mostly two-beat to five-beat lines, again mimicking the oceanic rhythms of the tides, their ebb and surge and thunderous "loud suck," augment that back and forth of both outer and inner tides. The sectioning of the poem adds to the effect in its almost diurnal mimicry of the tidal sea.

So yes, the very form and structure of this poem telegraph its difficulty—its complex intentions. Why? Because, as one delves deeper into it, the poem makes clear the complexity of the speaker's "vision." This is no fluffy descriptive poem; rather, it is a beautiful but severe rumination, a meditation, what Coleridge called a thought-poem, centering on both the cosmic and the personal. It is, in short, a lyrically rendered dramatic monolog—dramatic not in the sense of overt conflict between characters like that of the duke, duchess and envoy in Browning's poem, but in the sense of revelation, of thought both rational and metaphysical. No less than one of Hamlet's or Macbeth's or Lear's soliloquies, "On the Island" is not meant to comfort either the speaker or the spoken-to or the reader. It is meant to confront, to reveal, to challenge. This, too, is part of its complexity—why it is hard. To complicate things further, "On the Island" is a love poem—for the island and its beach, for the sea and for the spoken-to, for the "you" of the poem, maybe a woman, maybe a man, but either way a loved one.

Section one immediately establishes both the personal and metaphysical quandaries the speaker finds himself (an assumption, the gender) confronted with: his desire to express his love of his loved one's "ways" set against her (again, an assumption) "low mood"; and the stark polarities of life and death, of endless change, symbolized by the "tossed cemeteries of shells" and their "complex field<s> of monument and skeleton"—two stunning examples of Butler's complex imagery and metaphor. Indeed, if "On the Island" is by the end of just this first section announcing itself as hard, surely we realize already that it is a necessary hardness.

The second section expands thematically the first through two direct questions: How do waves begin? and Who can say why? We know, the speaker says, "how a sunk moon/ drains at the gut of the water," meaning its light, and the "reiterated argument" the wind in conjunction with tide and currents makes, and we know how that wind, by seizing on a "flaw" (of sea) "flags it bigger," creating the first wave, the "first snag from smoothness," meaning calm water—a wave "smaller than kisses" (another of those startling figures of speech). We know this, but who of us can say why? Trying to answer this question, he turns to mathematics, offering fractals as an explanation, but not himself a mathematician, he is neither at the "center of their thought" nor the "heart of the sea," so he can't testify to the validity of fractals as an answer.

The second section, then, continues and expands the metaphysical argument—basically, by establishing the limits of human knowledge. Just as he can't understand his loved one's shift of mood, so too the speaker can't the mystery of the natural world, both temporal and cosmic. Are both merely reflections of a universal entropy, uncontrollable and impervious to human reason? Or are they Chaos Theory in action—patterns of an underlying order where none seems apparent? If Butler's language and imagery seem at times to resemble Hopkins' ("catches a flaw and flags it bigger," "first snag from smoothness"), his mood and outlook resemble that of Arnold in "Dover Beach," or of Hardy in his more acerbic, probing poems. The questions the speaker is asking demand that level of language and vigorous attention—that level of difficulty. Hard art, indeed.

Straight-ahead narratives reach an inevitable climax, and meditative poems, in which the action is mostly internal, are no different. In "On the Island" the climax occurs in section three. It begins with the speaker saying he is "a man treading a thin shore," and beyond the literal seashore itself, he means language, the "hushed concussion of a million tongues/ in the fuzzy rush of a single phrase" (the assonance here a prime example of Butler's astute musicality) not able to provide the answers he is looking for, his human tongue suffering an injury, just as each successive wave suffers a "glassy relapse," slipping back into the sea's "loud suck," leaving him unable to distinguish one wave from another.

So here the climactic moment *is* his realization that while his desire is to "see headlines/ announcing themselves from nowhere like angels of love," he knows that "green was always gone/ on the whirling skin of <his> desire to see it." Green refers back to the "silver-green that ran/ the brassy tube of a rolling sunset" (Hopkins-like again, and a metallic allusion to earth, traditionally one of the four fundamental elements, the others being air, fire and water, all of which inform "On the Island"). But desire is not completion, not the fecund growth of knowledge symbolized by green he longs for. To his loved one he says he spoke "insistently to help <him> miss it"—"miss" double in its meaning, as "fix" is when he wonders if "that was what we were for,/ in double absence to fix the shimmer," a beautiful phrase, reflecting yet again Butler's mastery of image and musicality. As the water shimmers, so too does the knowledge that eludes him; he longs to fix—set/ correct—his understanding of the world, both inner and outer, so he no longer will miss perceiving it, no longer feel acutely its absence.

But what about language, that most elegant of human tools? Language, he asserts, allows him to name, to "enunciate," for example, the "hundreds of gulls and pelican, the heron," but up against the opacity of both the human heart and that of a vast non-human nature, he also realizes "how anything <he> says/ wheels away like a cry/ into the violent, empty sky." Devastatingly, the corollary to the limits of human knowledge is the limits of human language on which we so rely. This is the burden of the human condition. The speaker perceives the "shimmer," but paradoxically, can't arrest it into solid knowledge, even language, that beautiful codifier of sound and sense, not enough. This, above all, is his true epiphany—for a poet the most painful knowledge. Paradoxically again, however, the very human perception of the shimmer—of what can't be possessed—is itself a knowledge worthy of possession. Section four makes the case for this.

Awareness, even the most tenuous, offers, like language, "vectors of hope, surprise, attention." To his loved one the speaker says they said each other's name "over and over," but as "a tag or a sort of adverb," even the act of naming a qualified action. Then he poses another question: "What goes on in the sun?" Nuclear explosions go on, but that isn't what he means. After a day on the beach they return home, back to their everyday existence, "burned to a new awareness…but still no wiser." There it is again, the limits of what they can know; they are changed, "not fitting <their> skins exactly," but wisdom, real deep knowledge, still elusive. Then the speaker enumerates specific examples of the mundane reality they have returned to, "whiskey in glasses" and "bad reception." Even light, "its snows and sizzle of misspent photons," is wasted in their "swollen service" (a phrase that connotes both an infected servitude and ritual) to mundane worldly matters, which came about eons "before Proconsul/ uttered a sound that might have been like/ the word <they> agreed on, letting go: *Good*." Here the speaker has contextualized their specific human condition. He has presented it historically, Proconsul being an extinct genus of primates (not to mention a Roman provincial governor). Their mundane existence is nothing new. What else but to accept the limits of their knowledge by letting go, accepting their historically preordained condition? *Good* is all they can utter, language too limited in its provisions. Ironic, that *Good*, but not ironic either. Not at all.

So what now? If the quest for knowledge has foundered on the rocky shore of absolute human limitations, where does that leave the speaker? What will serve as his safe harbor? The fifth and final section, in providing answers to these questions, redeems some of those "misspent photons," and consequently the speaker and his loved one. There is a "slice" of light after all.

The speaker, unable to sleep, appeals to his loved one to let him "appear" to go alone "down/ to the astounding moon," which actually is providing those real "slices" of light "across the black glitter, impossible liquids" of the sea. There, imaginary as it is, while he has the satisfaction of "cold wet grit," of sand, under his feet and the "bite and moisture" of the air in his lungs, he realizes—gains knowledge—that nothing has ever made him as happy as "the greenest look" of his loved one when she believes he has made her happy; that look she has given him "should consume/ even the question/ of why we come to the sea to be puzzled." Love, he realizes, is everything—itself the knowledge above all other that is available to him.

And so, after his foray into both the inner and outer mysteries, after all the questions that have no answers, the speaker ends where he began, back with those waves, but "determined to see/ at least one surge all the way through/ with a simple spirit," and if not the first wave, or the second, then "antepenultimate, the third." One wave complete, one love entire.

So what, ultimately, is it that, for many readers, renders poetry so ruthlessly difficult? Certainly Butler's poem is not easy, demanding as it does exceedingly close attention to its form, its structure, its methodology, even its richly nuanced language. But forget for a moment its craft, its imagery and metaphors, its musicality—its sense of sound and sound of sense. Poetry like Butler's is a hard art, a necessary hard art, because it dares to plumb emotional, intellectual and metaphysical/spiritual strata, often paradoxically; and in "On the Island" the speaker's reaction itself is paradoxical: He's dazzled by the enormity of what he doesn't know, outwardly and inwardly, and simultaneously aggrieved by his inability to know—an ultimate, even cosmic, hard fact of our humanity.

True to the nature of things, human and otherwise, this is poetry's necessary hardness, too. When poetry embraces the limits of knowledge, and of language itself, imposed by our quotidian imperfection, it has the chance to be transcendent, to be a great poetry. We should, therefore, welcome necessary hardness, not disparage it out of vicissitude or fear. Only then, as in Jack Butler's amazing poem, does the hard art of poetry become truly revelatory—become true art.

* Permission granted by the author

What Makes a Poem a Master Work?

That, of course, *is* the question. There are all kinds of ways to answer it, from basic technique to the cumulative effect alluded to by Emily Dickinson when she talked about the top of her head coming off. Really, though, knowing a poetic master work is much like the old adage about pornography: You can't really define it (though we keep trying), but you know it when you see (read) it.

I have just read one: a poem titled "I Thought My Father Was Time" by Jack Butler:

I Thought My Father Was Time*

because he frightened me.
Spooky the cut of the yellow light as it crossed
the white wall of the one house I knew
with shadows of cottonstalk.
End of the day, and he would walk,
that thin man, home
from the tractor shop. All I could see
looking up from my play,
all that the long long light could show,
a struggle of stem and blue ghost,
his monstrous shadow writhing as he strode my way.

For all the times it happened, there was not one
I turned and looked into the sun.

Flight instructor, mechanic, plantation hand,
wild hair and youngest brother,
he'd married that slender brunette you see in all

    the forties movies, pure sex and steel
  but innocent as a glass of milk: my mother,
who fought his drinking to a standstill and made him change
    his Luckies for a pipe. War over,
   we lived as tenants on the family land
  all those slow undefined years, the middle range
   of the century, before the madness set in.

    Why do I dream him now
  as I saw him then?—Those inset blue pale eyes
    as pitiless, I thought, intolerant,
  as mine were weak, unclear. The lipless thin
   line of the mouth, the cruel hook of nose.

   Night after night on the battlefront
of being, a lean, then fat man haunts me, waits to see how
    long I go naked in church.

 It might have been he beat me, but he didn't, much.
    Once after a prank
   of pepper up his sleeping nostrils, a stunt
   I'd no doubt gotten from a cartoon.
  Oh he erupted grandly as any Katzenjammer
    uncle, but I had not foreseen
the trickster caught up in his trick like a broken plank
  in a whirlwind. Once when I lost his hammer.

   Dreaded, those whippings, unpleasant,
   but rare, and not unusual then. That wasn't
the reason. But he frightened me, frightened me long
    before he ever stood
  in a thunderous pulpit announcing how good

   could hardly bear the sight of evil
and so must hurl us down to that sulphurous level
    of never-ending flame, unless

we came down front before the song
concluded: *Almost, but lost…*

Talk about less than zero.
But to be fair, hellfire and brimstone were not
his major topics. He preferred the less
spectacular professions, taught
the gentle ministrations of *caritas,*
the operations of the Holy Ghost
(my favorite invisible superhero).

He frightened me, my father,
long before sex.

The first time I lost my virginity
I was soaping it up in a Louisiana bathtub,
and there it was, hard (rub-a-dub-dub),

and then there *it* was, another kind of lather.
Lucky I didn't get a complex—

the best he could explain,
was *You know how, when you need to pee
in the morning, it's stiff?
That's how it is when you love somebody.* His voice rough
with terrible shame. In the car, at night,
driving the Pontchartrain
causeway. I can still see the black water
out my window, the silent radio's green light,
and maybe I heard thereafter
someone sobbing under the silence while I slept,
some windblown girl with brown and auburn hair,
who hadn't known it would be so dirty,
who hadn't known it would be so bad.

Maybe I did

and maybe I didn't. Oh the demons crept
hobbling and hopping about the fire
till I was thirty,
until I learned that they were only
their own long shadows. True,
But that wasn't it.
Oh, that wasn't it.

He frightened me before I grew angry
and learned to curse
like a river of boiling music tearing along
full of tree-trunks and houses and bodies, before I knew
separate-but-equal was shit
and the war was wrong
and my country was twisted and sick and corrupt with power
and murdered the weak,
and said so, and said the Baptists were worse,
that he in his fried-chicken preacher fat
just sat in his recliner, sat
and kicked back and let it happen. So we didn't speak
for several years.

I thought my father was time because he frightened me,
and he frightened me to tears
this summer. Frailer than smoke
on the mountain, an old man gone lean

again, shade of that Air Force captain who took
my mother's heart, he was so glad to see
his prodigal son,
I thought for a moment his mind had gone,
he had forgotten my name,
his own. And in the next moment time
was rolled away,
and there he was at last: My father,
as real as anything.

And so we came together.
I sang for him in church, and he said,
I didn't know you could sing.
I put my hands to either side of his head
and held it, and he said, *Do that again.*

What can I say of the man?
His heart more fragile than a china vase.
His gaunt and stubbled face.
The uncommon grace
with which he met his death,
using his last breath,
when the heart attack bit,
to phrase, not the pain or doubt
I know he had, but to praise the life
he had been given: his path, his calling. His wife.

I thought my father was time, and never knew
time was my father, and my father's father.
Oh it was time that frightened me wild.

I am walking toward you out of that fire,
and I wouldn't bother
to speak these words, except that you
may still be watching some shadow on a wall,
and I want to say there's nothing to fear,
child,
nothing to fear.

* *Permission granted by author*

As the title indicates, the subject of this eighteen-stanza poem is the speaker's relationship with his father; so the theme of identities in collision is archetypal—necessary, I believe, to a masterful poem. It has to have large purpose. Further, equating the father with time itself is innovative, an original approach another necessary trait. Also, a master poem must be dynamic in time and space, not static, and the way Butler moves the poem along various points on the escalator we call time provides that dynamism. There is history—both event and biography—but there is also the dream/ nightmare unreality projected through a boy's deep-seated fear of his father. Of course, the structure of the poem, together with an unerring use of poetic technique, is absolutely essential. The structure must accommodate the progression of the poem and be contextually apt, which Butler achieves with stanzas of various lengths and a very functional meter and rhyme. Finally, and perhaps most subjectively, a masterful poem must be poetic, which is to say, it must possess a felicity of expression that leaves an indelible musical imprint on the memory.

Memory, as it turns out, is absolutely crucial to Butler's poem. It consists, after all, of childhood memories. Now a grown man, the speaker relates key moments with his father that span the years from childhood, when his father was "that thin man, home/ from the tractor shop" who to his boy self was a "monstrous shadow writhing as he strode [his] way," to his manhood when he found himself confronting his father's death, realizing that, while he had "thought [his] father was time," he "never knew/ time was [his] father." Time is both subject and structure. The various stanza lengths, the meter—two- to six-beat lines iambic but loosely so—and the just as variously indented lines effect the movement of time, both at its most staccato and fluid, which in turn lends to the dream/ nightmare imagery so crucial to the poem. Twice the speaker directly links time to his fear of his father, telling us he thought his father was time "because he frightened me." Fear of the father is linked to fear of mortality, thus enlarging the father to a figure mythic in proportion, which even physically to a small boy is why his father would appear a "monstrous shadow." The father didn't walk toward the boy; he "strode," a verb conveying strength and purpose, fearfully so. The boy is fixated, so afraid he not once turned away and "looked into the sun," the source of light and warmth. He is that traumatized. Clearly, by the end of the first two stanzas the speaker has equated the father with death—mortality. Clearly, too, the poem is operating both on a personal and more universal level, its themes truly archetypal: the complexities of a father/son relationship, identity and the fear of mortality, as they play themselves out over time.

Structurally, the poem can be divided into six sections, the first of which comprises the opening three stanzas. The third stanza establishes a quick family biography, defining the father as a man of various skills—flight instructor, mechanic, plantation hand—and introducing the mother as "pure sex and steel/ but innocent as a glass of milk," a compelling image of contradiction: a woman straight out of the "forties movies" who fought her husband's drinking "to a standstill" and "made him change/ his Luckies for a pipe." We learn the family "lived as tenants on the family land" during the middle years of the century, "before the madness set in." Butler's use of ambiguity here is perfectly placed: Whose madness? The father's? The mother's? The speaker's, driven by fear?

The next six stanzas, section two, answer the question, but the answer itself is ambiguous. The speaker wonders why he still dreams his father the way he "saw him then," as a boy: "pitiless," "intolerant," "thin line of the mouth," "cruel hook of nose." The fear he felt in the presence of his father is palpable. He summarizes this with a memorable war image, "the battlefront of being." The speaker says his father, once thin then fat, "waits to see how/ long [he goes] naked in church," the word "church" foreshadowing what we learn about the father farther along in this section: that he is a preacher. The speaker, as a boy, felt as if his father was lying in wait for him, ready to pounce once the boy was vulnerable—"naked"—enough. That the father was physical in his anger is made clear in the rest of this section, but with a qualification: "It might be he beat me, but he didn't, much." That comma before "much" reminds one of Browning's "I call that piece a wonder, now," in "My Last Duchess," again demonstrating Butler's craftsmanship. While the speaker eschews the notion of his father as a boy beater, that "much" qualifies his own assertion. Clearly, his father whipped him, once for losing a hammer, and left the boy, ironically, a "trickster caught up in his trick like a broken plank/ in a whirlwind." The simile is apt and powerful, again illustrative of Butler's acute technical expertise. So the father's anger manifests itself along a spectrum that includes his "erupt[ing] grandly" to whippings that were "unpleasant,/ but rare" and culturally "not unusual then" to the father as preacher "in a thunderous pulpit" warning in true Jonathan Edwards fashion of hellfire and brimstone, from which even confessing one's sins wasn't enough: "Talk about less than zero." Yet the speaker again qualifies the picture of the father he has given us: "That wasn't the reason," he says, his father frightened him, his fear predating all of it. He says his father preferred "less spectacular subjects," teaching "caritas"—charity, compassion—and the "operations of the Holy Ghost"—the speaker's "favorite invisible superhero," a ghost ironically distinct from "blue ghost," as he earlier described his father.

Section three, comprised of the next three stanzas, immediately announces its thematic focus: sex. This section achieves a lyricism driven by memory. Following the first two-line transition stanza, which reasserts the speaker's fear of his father and pre-dates it "long before sex," the second stanza is an intimate description of his loss of virginity, by masturbation, "soaping it up in a Louisiana bathtub." This stanza segues into the third with his father explaining that "when you love somebody" the penis grows erect, as it does in the morning "when you need to pee." This, too, is an intimate father/ son moment, but because the father (his voice) is "rough/ with terrible shame," until he is thirty the speaker is consumed with guilt, the "demons [creeping]/ hobbling and hopping about the fire." There is no doubting Butler's lovely musicality, his felicity of expression, in the bulk of the two stanzas when the speaker describes riding with his father in their car at night, "driving the Ponchartrain":

> I can still see the black water
> out my window, the silent radio's green light,
> and maybe I heard thereafter
> someone sobbing under the silence while I slept,
> some windblown girl with brown and auburn hair,
> who hadn't known it would be so dirty,
> who hadn't known it would be so bad.

That discordant "dirty" and "bad" are all the more grating and effective in such a lyrical context. The speaker isn't sure of his own knowledge of sin at that moment, not until later in life when he learned that the demons "were only/ their own long shadows." But again, Butler closes out the section with the speaker reasserting that none of that was the reason he feared his father. Or why he dreamed of the girl. There's that ambiguity again, the speaker's fundamentally conflicted view of his father, and of himself.

Talk about dynamic, as the poem shuttles backward and forward in time it seems as if we are observing the speaker in regression. Section four begins with his assertion that his father frightened him, not only before sex, but "before [he] grew angry/ and learned to curse/ like a river of boiling music," another stunningly original and evocative image—cursing, specifically, at the events of the 60's: "separate-but-equal was shit" (Civil Rights); "that the war was wrong" (Vietnam); that his "country was twisted and sick and corrupt with power" (The Establishment); and that the "Baptists were worse" (Hypocritical Religion), especially his father who, "in his fried-chicken preacher fat…/ in his recliner, sat/ and kicked back and let it happen." So the Generation Gap caught them up and they "didn't speak/ for several years." Then, in the second of this three-stanza section, everything changes. It opens with the speaker repeating the opening line of the poem, but then he adds, "and he frightened me to tears/ this summer." The speaker feared his father because his father had introduced him to mortality; worse now, his father has become his own case study. He is dying. What is so devastating to the speaker, however, is that this "old man gone lean again" and "frailer than smoke," this old man who "took [his]mother's heart"—this old man was "so glad to see/ his prodigal son" that the son "thought for a moment his mind had gone." How touchingly ironic, and painfully acute. Here he is, an old man who couldn't remember his own or his son's name, and in a flash "time/ was rolled away," and "at last" his "father,/ as real as anything"—not just a spooky, fearful demon stalking his son's real and dream life, but a man, a real man, a real father. The third stanza is simply a tender description of their having "[come] together," him singing for his father in church, the father realizing his son could sing, and finally, this:

> I put my hands to either side of his head
> and held it, and he said, *Do that again.*

Again, Butler's use of ambiguity marks this as a master poem. What does his father mean? Sing again? Or hold his head again? Or both? the ambiguity itself heightens the tenderness of this passage.

Section five, in its first stanza, testifies to the father's "uncommon grace/ with which he met his death," of a heart attack, by using "his last breath" to express "not the pain or doubt" the speaker "know[s] he had," but to "praise the life/ he had been given," both the path he had taken—his "calling" (avocation)—and "His Wife." Tellingly, "His Wife" is separated from the list to which it belongs by a period—she is special, most important to him. But of course it also is a fragment, mirroring perhaps their earlier described difficult married life. Once again, this is Jack Butler the superb poetic technician. Finally, then, in the second stanza of this section the speaker's epiphany is complete: He realizes now that his father wasn't time; rather, time was his father, and his father's father. He realizes that it was the passing of time that "frightened [him] wild." It was time that brought him mortal terror, not his father.

The last stanza of the poem constitutes the sixth and final section, and while one initially might see it as almost sentimentally apt, it really is not sentimental at all. The realization it expresses has been hard-won and is, after all, conditioned by loss—the loss implied by years of the speaker fearing his father for something he wasn't, and the actual physical loss of his father, and its corollary, the loss of the opportunity to share his new-found knowledge with him, and to act on it. The earlier fire imagery (the demon, the Edwards-like hellfire and brimstone) is drawn on again, but this time the speaker is "walking toward you out of that fire." He has been freed, but not necessarily so the "you" he is addressing, who "may still be watching some shadow on a wall." The "you" is of course the speaker's own child self, which is a brilliant strategy—this shift in point-of-view. It is daring and absolutely right. The section and the poem closes with the adult speaker telling his child self that "there's nothing to fear," then emphasizes his own hard-earned knowledge by adding, "nothing to fear at all."

Large purpose. Innovation. Dynamism. Technique. Felicity of expression—all of these must, as I hope has been demonstrated, be present in order to elevate a poem into a master work. They are, however, only the nuts and bolts. Ultimately, it is the blend of these that elevate, which makes a poem memorable. Certainly this amazing poem of Jack Butler's qualifies. But is the technical blend enough? Memorable is one thing, a master work another. And a great poem? Still another. Except in rare cases, whether a poem is great or not only time—history—can determine. A master work, however, is open to more immediate discernment. But even so something more than a blend of essential elements must be present, which perhaps is a bit more subjective, but still manifest. What Butler's poem, at least for this reader, has is that ineffable something that elicits an overwhelming emotional, intellectual, empathetic and in the end aesthetic response. Without this, a poem can be good in an ordinary sense, but not a master work. Call it a sublimity, a beautiful fusion of language and human intent, that lifts both the poem and the reader. Some might say, spiritual. But the sublime is a purely aesthetic ideal that all art aspires to, no matter the appellation one settles on. A master work achieves it, in some measure if not totally. Totally would be perfection, and that is an ideal of a whole different order.

For this reader, then, these remarks constitute an answer, even if only partial, to the question posed at the beginning. For this reader, Jack Butler's "I Thought My Father Was Time" is a poem that embodies that answer. It is a master work by one of our contemporary master poets. I, for one, am grateful for the poet and the poem.

Up Against Time: Physics & the Poem

Although certainly more than once was the case, most people probably don't think of physics and poetry as being complementary, and perhaps justifiably so. It is, after all, hard to relate the chaotic, random realm of quantum mechanics to the structured, orderly realm of poetry. At most, one could assert that poetry does try to get at the chaos *within* the human heart and psyche, much as quantum theory does the chaos underlying what's *out there*—outside the self. This said, there is one concept clearly relatable to both—time.

Einstein theorized that time is relative, both to position and motion. And so it is. Time and its measurement are variable. That being so, time is always unfixed in any definitive way, thus timeless. It is both changeable and changeless. Yet we humans change over what we call time. We change and then eventually we encounter the ultimate change, death, after which, except for the atoms of which we're made, we in a sense are changeless "for as long as forever is" (Dylan Thomas).

This brings us to poetry—specifically, to a poem by Jack Butler, the beautifully-wrought lyric "Lost Road Blues": *

Nobody here but me and the words, so I can say
what I want to how I need to to keep away
the mortal X-caliber blues.

You haunted me two hours in the rain,
Frank Stanford, yesterday. That empty pain
which jigs and rips and screws,

that vacuum, that why, and why, and why keep on,
that insupportable sway and creak and groan
before the pilings break.

I am the fire on the field, you said, or might have said.
I am the razor at your throat, the blood on your head,
the rust of shadows, the kingsnake

dressed as lightning, the smoke in the cotton patch.
I had been reading that special issue, natch
—oh the low funereal tone,

the memorial, dismal, and eloquent praise.
You'll generate your share of these essays,
I think, as time goes on.

I threw the magazine out the window of my van
on the way home later. No doubt you were the man,
the actor without fear.

I hope you got what you wanted from your few seconds of dying,
good buddy. But you don't help me. I'm just trying
to keep on breathing here.

"Road" of course implies journey, one type of which has an endpoint—"home"—and the other none, which in turn implies timelessness. "Lost" augments both types, in that it implies on the one hand an endpoint, if the speaker can but locate it in time and space, and on the other, no endpoint for him to locate, hence timelessness. "The Blues" alludes, also implicitly, to the music of the poem—the rhyme and prosody playing out through its eight stanzas—and to the psychic and emotional condition of the speaker as he participates in one journey (driving toward home) and confronts the implications of the other (moving inexorably into no-time, nothingness, death).

Like the notion of time itself, the poem is both constraint—its structure, its tightly-controlled tercets, its meter—and openness—its various line lengths as it unravels stanza after stanza down the page, and its stanza-interlocking third-line rhymes against the backdrop of each stanza's first two lines, each a rhymed couplet. These opposites directly mirror time and its opposite, timelessness.

Butler immediately bookends the poem in temporal time with the repeated word "here." The journey along the road is in the present, and the speaker is alone: "Nobody here but me and the words." So the journey is not shared. He is alone, in his van we later discover, with only "the words," which we also soon discover are those of another poet, and by implication his own, and so can say what he both wants and needs to "to keep away/ the mortal X-caliber blues." His quest, as the metaphor makes clear, is to fend off the blues, "mortal" signifying an acute awareness of fatality, of his own mortality, both physical and emotional, even spiritual. "X-caliber," an allusion of course to another quest, that of King Arthur and the sword in stone, suggests an epic, mythical quest, but the spelling denotes the caliber of a firearm, an image of deadliness. The speaker's temporal journey is one heightened by mortal stakes.

The second stanza establishes a more immediate reason for the speaker's bout with the blues: He recalls being "haunted... two hours in the rain" the day before by the late poet Frank Stanford. In the rest of the stanza, and the third, the speaker, confronted by the fact of Stanford's now eternal absence, his death, addresses "That empty pain/ which jigs and rips and screws" (a viciously active verb-melodic line), then asks "why, and why, and why keep on," the repetition expressive of the haunting and the speaker's despair. He is bemoaning the sense-lessness of existence, of going on through time, of persisting in the maw of timelessness, synopsizing his despair with the image of a pier, its sway and creak and groan/ before the pilings break." If that's the way the mortal journey ends, in empty timelessness, the journey itself is anything but comforting or easy. What, then, is the point?

In the fourth and ending with the first line of the fifth stanza, the speaker quotes what Stanford "said, or might have said," each citation presenting images of violence, of destruction, or potentially so: fire, razor, blood, rust, kingsnake, lightning, smoke. Then, in the rest of the fifth stanza and the next, he reveals that he's been reading a "special issue," a magazine containing essays of "low funereal tone," of "memorial, dismal, and eloquent praise," asserting that "as time goes on" Stanford will "generate [his] share of these essays."

The question arises: Are the essays actually that depressing in their praise, or is their description more accurately a reflection of the speaker's own depression, "lost" as he is on the road of his own mortal journey through time? Possibly, both. In any case, in the penultimate seventh stanza he throws "the magazine out the window of [his] van/ on the way home," an act of utter rejection and quasi-despair—quasi because of what follows.

In the eighth and last stanza the speaker asserts, almost accusatorily, that he hopes Stanford "got what [he] wanted from his few seconds of dying...." This, after ambiguously conceding that Stanford was "the man,/ the actor without fear." Admiring, yes, but damning, too: he was, after all, an actor, and his lack of fear an act—a mask. Here, too, a question arises: Is Stanford the only actor? The only one who dons a mask?

"Lost Road Blues" closes with the speaker firmly stating that Stanford—his example and his poetry—doesn't help him in his own mortal journey through time, that he's "just trying/ to keep on breathing here" (the feminine rhyme of "dying" and "trying" qualifying the very effort he is making). He's trying to stay alive, to keep on moving along that lost road, the movement through time itself a "momentary stay" (Frost) against its opposite, no-time.

Time, timelessness, mortality, death. Structurally, the way Butler has enclosed the timeless, the infinite, the endpoint of the temporal within the parentheses of the temporal—the present, the now, what we call time—is telling. Confronted with the "rust of shadows" and all the other lurking terrors of the timeless, the speaker resists. He chooses to "keep on breathing," just as this acute lyric does throughout its mellifluous march down the page, stanza unto stanza, sometimes panting hard from the exertion, sometimes rhythmically and gently, even as the pilings crumble.

In this resistance, itself an act of will, of choice—in this, futile though it ultimately proves to be, there is embedded a hope, and in the hope a human nobility. Though the poem bemoans the mortality we all are subject to, it praises our insistence on resistance, our embrace of time, even as we acknowledge its opposite, timelessness.

* Permission Granted by Author

Poet, Jack Butler

Oz

And the Flood Flowers Now: On the Trail of the First Hippie

Especially when the wind comes skidding in from the bay and punishes your skin it really is the end of the world—more so on a moody, misty, drizzly day such as the one when I arrived. Laugharne: a snip of a Welsh town made known to the world by a honey-tongued boozer of a son who left its isolation once too often. His last trip back was in a box.

I went there in the summer of 1980 to establish for myself the concrete fact of him and it, the poet and his town. In many ways it's difficult to love the legend of the man, fleshed as it is with so much pain. That pain still lingers. You can sense it in the voices of the Welsh themselves, those who remember. They've made an industry of their wayward poet son, but ask them what they think of him and venom's what you get, at least from some.

For instance, in Cwmdonkin Park, in Swansea, where the Thomas myth begins, I talked to the park ranger, a man in his sixties, with a Hitler-like mustache and rosy cheeks. I asked him if he'd known young Dylan. "No," he said, "An' thank the Lord! I wouldn't of 'ad 'im in any part of my 'ouse, that one. A waster an' a boozer, he was—one of them 'ippies. An' 'is wife, too, though she's a nice lady now. The Welsh 'ave no use for 'im; it's you people 'ave made 'im what he is."

And there's some truth in that. Thomas *was* a hippie—was, minus the long hair, tie-dyed shirts, beads and hallucinogens—an illustration of the term long before it evolved. His misbehaving still was talked about, disdainfully or, at best, with awe for his prodigious carousing. When I was looking for his cottage in New Quay, where Thomas spent a year or so during the War, I asked an elderly lady at the Tourist Information booth where it might be. She instructed me to turn left at the Black Lion pub, where, she said, "he'd lived most of the time." It was subtle, but the snide distaste was there, as well, I suspect, as a kind of perverse pleasure in setting straight the record for a starry-eyed American hungry for a literary hero and, in her view, all too ready to ignore the truth. And when I'd found the Black Lion and its owner, a beefy-faced man with a beefy body who used, he said, to live in Buffalo and had been a boxer (brandishing his fists), he became very voluble on learning I was chasing Dylan Thomas and his legend, telling me how Thomas had "lived" in the Black Lion for two years and how he had a commemorative plaque in the pub and how he'd tell me all about him if I'd come that evening. That he knew a lot about Thomas the pub-crawler I had no doubt. But drinking stories weren't what I was looking for, so that was that.

I never did find the cottage, and, despite the sometimes outright disapproval of Thomas and his "ways," my gut impression was that, deep down, the Welsh admire the very eccentricity they so excoriate. At the very least, they probably have a fellow countryman's pity for a man who, by the end of his life, was so obviously ill. As the old seaman I met at New Quay said, when I asked for his help in plotting my next day's route, "We're only on this earth for a short while, and that's what we're here for, to help each other." A pity Thomas was beyond such help. In the end even Wales couldn't keep him safe. Nor could his great gift.

But perhaps that's not so important now. Sixty-five years ago his wife Caitlin brought his bloated body back to Wales and laid it in a simple grave and marked it with a simple wooden cross in the newer section of the graveyard of St. Martin's Church, a thirteenth-century structure in the common Celtic shape of a cross. In the church's information pamphlet I was told that Thomas was the most famous person buried in the graveyard, that he was "renowned throughout the world." You'd never know it, though, to look at the grave itself. The cross was white, its only distinction being that it was the only wooden one. It was clearly visible from the road and, set among so many headstones, seemed as frail as its designee was in life. The only time-defeating strength in Thomas was his gift. On the cross, of course, were the by then much-photographed and-printed words IN MEMORY OF DYLAN THOMAS WHO DIED ON NOVEMBER 9, 1953. As I knelt by his grave, which was rounded high in the Welsh fashion, I noticed, just in front of the cross at the base, two seashells. Turning one over, I found a maggot "leeching like time" to the underside. Though it appalled me, it was fitting for a poet in whose work we find such images of death and decay. On looking up, I saw, stretched from the left arm of the cross to its base, a spider web, the universal image of dread, the spider nearly invisible, lost in its own artifice. On such a gray day it seemed almost too poetically apt. Rearranging the little flowers in their jar, the only decoration on the grave, I quickly rose and went my way.

Many people have referred to Dylan Thomas as a great drunk. I disagree. He wasn't a great drunk; drink helped to murder him. Had he been a great drunk he would have lived a lot longer. He would have managed his drinking rather than it managing him. The only parts of Thomas still extant are his words. Perhaps he was a great poet. I don't know. I do know that he wrote some great poems. Maybe that's enough. It is for me. And certainly it is for others. That's what's important, even more so after sixty-five years. The pain still lingers, but the gift gives life. At least that's what Mrs. Muriel Davies, the elderly woman who, since 1939, had lived in Thomas's childhood home at 5 Cwmdonkin Drive in Swansea, said: "He has enriched my life." Meaning, of course, his words, his gift of life. Of this there was no doubt. One look at her told you that. It was in her eyes and in her heart, deciphered by a sprightly tongue.

Eighty if a day and all crumpled and twisted, Mrs. Davies had two canes for a recently injured leg and for a generally weakened condition. Just to look at her was wrenching, and you knew her days were "winding down now/At God speeded summer's end." And yet, in chatting with her in the parlor for an hour, I heard nothing in her voice but gratitude and eagerness and love of life and poetry and Dylan Thomas and his world. Among other things I learned that, since she and her husband had moved into the house, they had made themselves custodians of the Thomas myth. Signed books of critics who had benefitted from their help testified impressively to that, as well as the letter from Thomas dated, if I remember correctly, 1946, in which he'd thanked her husband for his fine calligraphy accompanying a book he'd put together of some of Thomas's works. Her pride was evident. Yet the legend hadn't taken over, either. She'd redone the house inside, because "it was so ugly," painting over the garish blues and greens and reds with softer tints. She said she liked to talk to Thomas "addicts," but that she always warned them that the house was her "home and not a museum." And so the gift goes on, although the poet doesn't. No one need ever defend that artist as a young dog to Mrs. Muriel Davies.

So, as with Swansea, I'd come to Laugharne to find the Wales the poet said he'd held in his arms. And it was still there, though tamed in some ways by the times. The town was unchanged, as far as I could tell, from what the townsfolk said and from the books I'd read, except of course for surface alterations. The castle, "brown as owls," was in 1980 undergoing rehabilitative work to make it fit for tourists and their pocketbooks, and in the window of the bookshop, displayed prominently, were several books by and about Thomas, his work and his life. In the restaurant where I stopped for a hot mug of coffee, I saw one of those cheap paintings, garishly colored, of Thomas in his curly-headed twenties, an imitation of the famous Augustus John portrait. Truly, though too late for the poet, the flood had flowered. Still, despite the rather mild invasion of tourists for that time of year (July and August), Laugharne was as it always was: a small Welsh village nestled on Carmarthen Bay. The wind still chilled, the tides still rose and fell, and the "cry of seagull and rook" still trembled in ears turned toward the bay.

Surprisingly, given Thomas's fame, the little niche of Laugharne that was his was also pretty much unchanged, again despite the tourists and the literary pilgrims like me who came seeking all that was left of his actual life: his "house on stilts" and the shack above it where he worked and, at the end, tuned his despair to the rhythm of the sea. To get there you still had to make the trek along what the locals called Dylan's Walk; you still had to turn your collar up against the sea-sprayed wind; you still had to stop along the way, awed by the panoramic bay and Sir John's Hill, the seagulls piercing you with their unearthly shrieks.

The shack surprises, too. It's such a tiny thing, so frail against the big blue bay. The sign above the door informs you that it's real, however, so you tiptoe up and peek in through the glass. Inside you find that everything appears to be the way it was the day he left "for as long as forever is." But how, you wonder, could the sheets of paper on the table and, on the wall, the snapshots of his poet heroes still be crisp and unyellowed after so many years? The answer arrives with the fee-collector and her key: a documentary by the BBC. It's on to the boathouse, recently purchased by some group or other and run now as a memorial and center for the arts. Inside, while a recording of his works being read by actors keeps you company, you move from room to room inspecting art exhibits, newspaper clippings and photographs of him, his family and his work. At the end you talk to the fee-collector, buy a postcard or two, take one last look, and leave. You don't look back.

I'd come to Laugharne, to Wales, to try to get a fix on Thomas, on his poetry. Somehow I wanted to shave away all the stubble, the shadow that was the myth entwined with that from which the legend sprang. I wanted my curly-headed cherub of a poet clean-shaven. I wanted his cheeks rosy in the sea salt wind of Wales that I might touch my cheek to his and say, "Aye, that's the rub that counts." Or, as I put it in a poem I'd promised to send to Mrs. Davies, I didn't want the rub to be a "slap and not a tickle." That's why I'd come. But, all these many years later, what I know I truly found was that the slap was tickle and the tickle slap. As Mrs. Davies, in her wisdom, knew, to long for otherwise is to become a curiosity in a museum of your own delusionary making. In a kind of unintended way, despite the beauty of its capture in his lovely poems, childhood and its camaraderie with traitor time (and later, alcohol and its camaraderie with true blue death) is the museum in which the poet Dylan Thomas lies encased and, like the spider on his white cross, lost in a thick web of his own words.

Thomas once said of the Swansea Museum that it looked as if it belonged in a museum. Perhaps those are fitting final words for the first hippie.

Lingering Sweetness: On the Road with George

In his preface to his book of essays, *Travels with George in Search of Ben Hur and Other Meanderings*, Paul Ruffin asserts that "Nobody reads prefaces." Perhaps not, but everyone ought to read these familiar and not so familiar essays.

For one thing, they are chock full of Southern gusto—in their language, their characters and their storytelling. Often all of this is served up with gut-busting humor. All one has to do, for example, is read "Workshopping a Cowboy Poem," which contains one of the most hilarious presentations of Yeats' "The Second Coming" ever put to paper. Or consider "Rats!" in which literal rats inhabiting Ruffin's Texas Review Press office are talking to each other about those weird human creatures. Talk about a shift in perspective! And not to be forgotten is "Just Thinking About Shit," a comedic consideration of that much-used word's lineage and its plethora of applications down through the centuries. It will leave any reader howling with delight at so much ado over…well, you know.

Except for "Rats!" these essays all appear in the first of three sections that comprise the book, Things Literary, More or Less, and indeed we do encounter such notables as George Garrett, Eudora Welty, Emily Dickinson, Edgar Allen Poe, Theodore Roethke and, for this reader most unforgettably, Ernest Hemingway. Ruffin is, after all, a much respected reader, critic, writer and editor. So one would expect such familiarity. But these essays are about more than encounters with the literary; they are, always, about Paul Ruffin: his character, his Southern roots, his Texas and Mississippi and Alabama, his personal history, and most tellingly, his honesty—expressed in a language that is both directly literal and metaphorically lyrical. Consider this passage, just one of innumerable examples:

> The sparks from the fire sprang up into the stars,
> and the stars fell into the fire, and I was seeing six

boys instead of three and two moons instead of one.
After a few more swallows, which I managed to
prop myself up for, everything went as black in my
head as those night woods.

This excerpt is from "Drinking: A Truncated History," the essay that leads off the second section, "On Likker and Guns." It is a personal favorite precisely because it demonstrates beautifully Ruffin's lyrical and narrative honesty. In it he recounts right up front his long history with alcohol, all the ramifications "likker" has had in his life. Certainly some of this is painful, for him and for all of his readers who recognize the common thread of drink and its effects in our own lives; how something so potentially injurious in so many ways is also elevated into a uniquely American mythos. Yet, couched in the downhome, ass-kicking colloquial stew Ruffin lays out, it also is hilarious. Read the last few pages of the essay and there will be no doubt. How one afternoon he got drop-dead drunk on Heaven Hill and his recounting of it has to be one of the funniest descriptions of a one-day binge ever written.

Humor, then, is one very large weapon in Ruffin's literary armament. It sometimes bubbles gently and ironically, at others erupts like geysers. It is, demonstrably, potent. But don't be fooled. Again, this author also has an intense lyricism that conveys a deep undercurrent of emotion, very often a kind of cascading tenderness. Read "The Girl in the Clean, Well-Lighted Place," his homage to a great short story and its author and in the setting and characters and mood it evokes, his rendering of it. Loneliness is at the heart of it, and its concomitant sense of nothingness ("nada pues nada"); that acute crippling sense of meaninglessness at the core of human existence. But, by the end, like Ruffin, one understands that while "you don't know any more about life than you did before you went in," you also understand that "you're not so lonely anymore and the road doesn't seem as long." Through suffering you come to realize that "sometimes lonely is not bad because lonely teaches you to appreciate the things and people in your life that keep you from *being* lonely." Here, and in other pieces, Ruffin's achievement is that kind of lyricism; that kind of tenderness.

In the third section, *Growing Up in Mississippi Poor and White but*

Not Quite Trash, Ruffin also displays that intense lyricism. In the first of two excerpts from his not yet published memoir, "Trains: The Beginning of a Lifelong Quest for Understanding," he basically presents us with his lifelong love of trains, another American mythos, and in doing so, tenderly recalls his grandfather. Specifically, he recollects lovingly how his grandfather met the trains night and day with his little cart to tote the mailbags from the depot to the post office. At the end of the essay, he describes a "small glass engine" his father had given him, "its smokestack filled with small hard candies, reds and greens and yellows." Ruffin writes he ate one daily for weeks. More than just candy, he says, the taste reminded him "of trains and the worlds they came from and went to."

Similarly, the essays in this, his fourth collection, become symbolic of much larger worlds than the often insular Southern world they describe. That is their true significance, their true gift—the gift Ruffin has given his readers. As such, like those small hard candies, they leave us with a "lingering sweetness." Like the candies, they are rock-hard and real; and like them, they are the real transformed by the imagination into dreams.

Near the end of "The Girl in the Clean, Well-Lighted Place" Ruffin writes half wistfully and half determinedly, "But it cannot end here, whatever magic has been at work." He needn't have worried. In this wonderful book of essays he has made certain that, to quote the Houston journalist Leon Hale whom he quotes in his preface, his tales "start<s> off as truth and… go<es> on that way a long time." This too is magic.

Author and editor, Paul Ruffin.

Just Like Oz: The Making of a Book

(The Horse's Name Was Physics)

In his book *Infinite in All Directions,* Freeman Dyson writes: "Anyone who tries to explain modern science to the general public faces a choice, either to write an elementary textbook with technical terminology carefully defined, or to take refuge in metaphor. I have chosen the latter course." So have I. But in my case there was no choice. I am not a scientist, except perhaps in my fantasy life, and most certainly I am not a mathematician. Hardly. What science I know I achieved through the reading of scientists who have mastered metaphor, like Freeman Dyson.

So I have no real credentials. I am, like everyone, defined by what I know and what I don't. Those are my only qualifications. Philosophically I hold with Bohr: Complementarity is everything and everything-not, is wave and not-wave. Complementarity is the double helix of my universe, metaphor its rendering.

Metaphor is the molecular replication of language. It is an image locating its double, or its double locating it. The double we call a comparison. It might not be as exact as the language of science—mathematics—but in the right hands it can be as elegant as the double helix itself. It will come as no surprise to biologists if I say that metaphor anchors itself, by and large, in the natural world. That is its strength. It is a bridge between two worlds. It might be made merely of rope and might sway in the fierce wind of the imagination, but it is crossable. More to the point, it is open to anyone, the only toll exacted that of appreciation and a willingness to forge ahead. Certainly many scientists used it. Besides Dyson, there was Einstein atop his light beam and standing in his train depot. How many of us would understand relativity otherwise? There was Rutherford with his flies banging around inside cathedrals. And Loren Eisley. And Carl Sagan.

And Gary Zukav. These men and so many others have led me through the wonders of the universe. And they have done it with metaphor.

But it began with Michelangelo. In 1986 I started work on a book of poems that focused on the life and work of this Florentine master of paint and stone. In the time it has taken me to complete that book, *The Hand that Rounded Peter's Dome,* I have learned much in the way of bringing character and concept to life—through direct narration, monolog, and metaphor. I have, in short, learned how to tell an epic story without writing an epic poem, a genre that doesn't seem congenial to our time, or that to which our time is not congenial. So struggling with my book on Michelangelo taught me the natural drama of character.

Then, in the summer of 1987, I stumbled on a book that told the epic story of our century. I read Richard Rhodes' splendid *The Making of the Atomic Bomb.* As I read, I began to realize I had come upon another whole world of characters just begging for poetic transmutation. I felt like Dorothy right after her entrance into Oz. In fact, the rich cast of characters and the story of the development of quantum mechanics itself was just like Oz. I was hooked.

The canvas grew, enlarging everything. I soon enough saw my own dilemma: this outrageous cast of characters, their natural drama, was the drama of the history they were so busy making. What had started as a human drama soon evolved into something much larger, a specific and yet abstract artifice produced by the likes of Moseley, Rutherford, Chadwick, and all the rest. Its structure, conceived in the 19th Century, was fashioned in the 20th. There was relativity. There was the Uncertainty Principle. There was fission. And there was the grand finale: Los Alamos and Little Boy.

In his book Dyson says Einstein said: "Scarcely anyone who has fully understood this theory can escape from its magic." And wasn't it Chadwick who, having heard that fission was sustainable, said years later that he hadn't had a good night's sleep since?

I've slept, but I, too, haven't escaped the magic.

It didn't take me long to realize I'd need an altar for those flies in the cathedral to rally to, something greater than the characters themselves. After all, with such a wonderful cast I could easily have written a book on any one of them. There were too many yellow bricks for even Oz. Then it hit me. The drama, the real story, was the physics—all the work, the luck, frustrations, brilliance, breakthroughs. The science and the scientists were one. Seizing on this led directly to my own breakthrough.

And it, of course, came back to metaphor.

I determined to focus on the moment of creative insight, when the scientist and poet braid themselves together into helix, stitch themselves into the fabric of the universe; or, to extend my earlier metaphor, when they cross the swaying rope bridge into the zone where God both plays with dice and doesn't. Call it inspiration: that one moment when the poet and the scientist are the double origin of everything.

Like Heisenberg, for instance. There's that moment on a late March night when he's out walking on the soccer field behind Bohr's Institute. He looks up at the stars, through branches of the great beech trees, and suddenly he's there in Oz. Uncertainty. The randomness of deep-down things. He sees. And metaphor is born.

Or Szilard. He's standing on a street in London, near Southampton Row. He's waiting for the light to change. It does. He starts across the zebra stripes. One moment it's a street he's crossing, the next our rope bridge. By the time he's reached the other side and the light's changed again, he understands a chain reaction's really possible. He sees what can't be seen. And he's in Oz. He sees. And metaphor is born.

So I had my altar. Soon the flies began to organize their orbits, and the grand cathedral was abuzz. I'm reminded by Dyson of what Rutherford said to Eddington about electrons: "Not exist, not exist—why I can see the little beggars there in front of me as plainly as I can see that spoon."

Exactly. I can see them, too, the little beggars. But the trick is to have naysayers see them. All the doubting Eddingtons. There had to be a way of making the electrons visible. And of course there was. I soon saw that the very form of poems could reflect the drama of the concepts. Imagine, the structure of the poem itself was metaphor.

Consider Edward Teller. Rhodes says he was finally won over to commitment to the Bomb when he heard FDR speak in Washington.

And we all know the power of that man's tongue—the sheer, compelling power of the rhythms of his words. Teller was mesmerized into belief. And galvanized into his future "fatherhood": the hydrogen bomb. And what poetic form could mirror such a tongue? Could mesmerize through rhythms, repetitions, rhymes? The villanelle of course:

> You men must rally round the atom's might,
> he said that day, his voice bombarding us.
> You must not hesitate in this good fight.
>
> As soon as he began I saw the light,
> each sentence wrapping me in its embrace.
> I, too, must rally round the atom's might.
>
> And all of you, he said, must put to flight
> your doubts. The world is as it always was.
> You must not hesitate in this good fight.
>
> He speaks to me, I thought. And he is right.
> It's not our fault. The world is mad, not us.
> I, too, must rally round the atom's might.
>
> It's up to you, he said, to keep the light
> of freedom glowing in the dark. God knows,
> you must not hesitate in this good fight.
>
> Never, I swore. I, too, have seen the light
> of freedom snuffed. And lived to keep these vows.
> I, too, will rally round the atom's might.
> And will not hesitate in this good fight.

And Szilard again. Rhodes tells us he was pushing hard for patronage, specifically that of Lewis Strauss. Like all the other Eastern European physicists, scattered so far and wide before the anti-birth of Hitler's government, Szilard had mastered letter-writing and cablegrams. Einstein had referred to all these brilliant scientists, himself included, as birds of passage. Well, birds of a feather might flock together—but not always. What form could capture such a farflung flock? A cablegram of course:

TO: LEWIS STRAUSS
   c/o KUHN, LOEB ASSOCIATES

FOR TWO YEARS NOW MY DREAM HAD VANISHED STOP I'D GIVEN UP STOP BUT LIKE THE ELECTRON JUMPING BACKWARD FROM ITS OUTER SHELL THE DREAM IS MINE AGAIN STOP URANIUM HAS GIVEN WAY STOP YOU OF COURSE KNOW WHAT THIS MEANS STOP I LEARNED OF IT FROM WIGNER SICK IN PRINCETON STOP WHO GOT IT VIA THE INFIRMARY STOP WHICH GOT IT IN TURN FROM WHEELER ET AL IN NEW YORK STOP WHO LEARNED OF IT FROM ROSENFELD STOP WHO GOT IT FROM BOHR EN ROUTE ON THE ATLANTIC TO NEW YORK STOP WHO LEARNED OF IT FROM FRISCH IN COPENHAGEN STOP WHO GOT IT IN KUNGÄLV FROM HIS AUNT MEITNER STOP WHO HAD IT STRAIGHT FROM HAHN IN DAHLEM STOP WHO SAYS A CHAIN REACTION ISN'T POSSIBLE?
   SZILARD

And wouldn't this form, this staccato, *be* the chain-reaction all the birds were closing in on like a winter nesting ground?

So there it was. I, too, had arrived. I'd crossed the bridge—or, rather, camped out in the middle. Finally, the science *was* the poetry, became its own metaphor. And it had precedents as wondrous as the inner guts of things. Think for a moment of the concepts made of metaphor. For example, Schrödinger's cat in the box. And Bohr's liquid-drop model of the atom, his hopping electrons. Think again of Rutherford's flies in the cathedral. "There is a time…," Ecclesiastes says. Well, now there is space-time. And particles inside of particles. And stars collapsing into holes as black as Hitler's heart. And quarks. And symmetries. And superstrings. And us.

Whatever the stars might or might not have signified over the centuries, I thank mine for metaphor. To the imagination it's the shuttle flight right into Oz. That's what we're all about: becoming our own metaphor. In fact, language is all that keeps us from the totally discrete, from being small and insignificant particles banging around like bats in the attic of our separateness. There ought properly to be a tenderness between the poet and the scientist. Wasn't it Bohr who said an idea, or a theory, isn't anything if it's lodged always outside of language? That in fact an idea wasn't worth a damn if it could not be put into words?

Language gives visibility. Gives theories of the most profound sort bones and flesh by making images of them. Through metaphor, of course. But there is more. Arrange the images, the metaphors, into a system governed, like the universe, by fundamental forces and you have the power of the symbol. Move the symbols into galaxies of character and event and you have, finally, myth.

Myth is the unified field theory of the language spoken by real beings in a universe that might or might not be so real. So making myths is crucial to the rhapsody of human life, and we create them from the star stuff of our presence in the universe. And once created they, like Rutherford's electrons, are made obvious as spoons. Language X-rays them into shape. And shape, or form, is life. And life, as Dyson says, is God's great gift.

In Dante, Heaven's a bore. But "Always," as Dyson says, "when things are dull, something turns up to challenge us and to stop us from settling into a rut." Oz is never boring. We live in a universe that's yesterday today and in which futures wheel and deal with stellar disregard for us. All we have left is the ability to make the devil dance.

Welcome to Oz.

Behind the Curtain

Marble All the Way: The Poetry of Allen Hoey

Hail

In my copy of one of his books, Allen Hoey wrote, "With friends like you, who needs angels?" Now, I might reverse that and ask, "With angels like you, who needs friends?" Allen died in 2010, on June 16, Bloomsday. He was only fifty-seven. He is gone, but his wonderful first book remains, one of six collections he left us, plus three novels.

A Fire in the Cold House of Being was published in 1987, having been selected by Galway Kinnell as the 1985 winner of the Camden Poetry Award, courtesy of the Walt Whitman Center. Soon after its publication I wrote an essay, "Marble All the Way: The Poetry of Allen Hoey." It seemed to me that his was one of those rare first books, praiseworthy for its technical virtuosity, its wide range of subject matter and its embrace of language both sacred and profane.

What follows is that essay, with some things edited, some added, but substantially the same. I wrote it in the belief that Allen was a remarkable poet, and that his book was deserving of recognition beyond the norm for a first book, and that a few of the poems were simply luminous.

I still believe it.

In the very title of Allen Hoey's book—*A Fire in the Cold House of Being*—are the clues to the "shape of the whole," as well as to the individual poems and how to read them properly. Notice, there are, both overtly and by implication, all four of the elements: fire, and air and water (cold), and earth—a "house" being rooted to the earth by its foundation, just as we are by our flesh and blood and bones. And a house, of course, is a residence, both shaping and shaped by its tenants.

So there is the literal suggestiveness of this marvelous title, which was "suggested," Hoey tells us, by a passage from Oliver Sachs' *Awakenings*. And, as with all better titles, there's the metaphoric: the creative "fire," obviously; the existential, appropriately; and, most mystifyingly, the religious. In "Nocturne," one of the smaller lyrics, Hoey, having just described the "beautiful ailanthus" outside the window of his study as it appears on a cold winter night, asks:

> Is this
> all that there is, O Lord, is this the fullness?
> Your signature in the stilled sap,
> your voice in my son's startled crying?

The overriding question these poems raise is: Is this god the Christian God or something else? This, despite the Christian iconography recurring in the book. In other words, is this God literal or metaphoric? Is there, in fact, a choice? Therein is the mystification. Quite apart from all its other virtues, Hoey's book centers itself most wonderfully on God. In its totality, *A Fire in the Cold House of Being* attempts to answer—or rather, come to terms with—the question posed: Is this the fullness?

What we have here is a book of poems that dare to question God. And, as with all such books, the answers, such as they might be, are quite beside the point. It's how the question's asked that counts. And in this 1985 Camden Poetry Award-winning book—chosen, significantly, by Galway Kinnell, himself a poet of the sacred—it counts for very much indeed. The book, regardless of whatever lapses it might have—which any book that dares enough to risk in a big way will—is a collection that announces a new talent. Easy, overused words, I know. But, in this case, equally as easy to demonstrate.

Look at the sectioning of the book: There are three. Look at some of the epigraphs: "The question is not/ Does being have meaning/ But does meaning have being" (to the book—Rexroth); "Hell hath no limits, nor is circumscribed/ In one self place, for where we are is Hell" (to the first section—Marlowe); "Preise dem Engel die Welt..." (to "The Things of August"—Rilke); "It's certain there is no fine thing/ Since Adam's fall but needs much labouring" (to the third section—Yeats).

Look at the titles: "The Simple Truth About Snow," "Building a Fire," "The Vision," "Icon," "To Open the Eternal Worlds," "Cutting on Easter," God, While Creating the Birds Sees Adam in His Thoughts, "Sunday Rock," "Stargazing: Letter to a New Hampshire Friend," "Hymns to a Tree," "Fire in the Trees, " "The Left-Handed Marriage," "Fishing the Hudson," "Nocturn," "Toil," "Optima Dies" and "The Word."

And look, most crucially of course, at the poems themselves.

Notice, first, that both the opening poem, "The Simple Truth About Snow" (for Hayden Carruth—again, a telling link), and "The Bus to Common Center," the last poem in the book, are set in nature and, by about the halfway point, have "turned to God." Like Kinnell, Hoey makes love to God by making love to nature, and in doing so fuses them, fuses himself and them, and thereby sanctifies the impulse toward that God by forging such a trinity. And, since the "fire" is the creative, too, he is both Blake the maker of the forge, and is the forge itself, on which, like Blake, he shapes "Eternal Worlds," and thereby opens them:

> O, Blake, to feel that,
> feel at one as leaf to tree, tree to hill,
> shedding and receiving heat, sharing light,
> mindful of the whole not just the part. Soul
> not purified from body, no, but knit
> as pulse and artery, the liquid flow of fire.

For Hoey, the creative fire and the eternal are a double helix, twined together and inseparable throughout the book. They are his own genetic code. One doesn't doubt this, even when there are overt expressions of art's limitations, or the pain it of necessity engenders. "The Simple Truth About Snow," a graceful catalog of the cliches we use in describing snow and a recounting by the speaker of his panic driving in a storm one night, ends, "My eyes/ open wider then than simile can tell." Face to face with the ineffable, words won't come. But in the next poem "Building a Fire," a little sixteen-line lyric that does exactly what the title says, Hoey reminds us that, limitations notwithstanding, building a fire (a poem?) the right way makes a difference. After all, he says, "Why else/

spend this time building/ what so quickly burns away." In the question is the doubt committed artists, soon and late, must struggle with and, against which, they must shape at least a "momentary stay." But notice that the question's punctuated with a period. The question is its answer. "One could do worse than be a swinger of birches," Frost said so memorably. Hoey would add: "Yes, and we have no choice." If that were all, however, what we'd have, "as the planet spins/ and tips these acres further into night," is the cold warmth of stars. What we'd have is the cold comfort of Pascal's famous wager: Belief in God is good because the opposite is bad. Is that enough—for either God or Art?

Well, notice that the next two poems, small lyrics both, hint at this poet's answer to that most metaphysical of questions by turning—re-turning—our attention to the physical. In "Casting at Night," a poem about fishing for trout (and more), the speaker, through a lovely metaphor, explains,

>   this weighted line,
>
> buzzing back and forth, threads
> night behind me with the dim
> vocabulary of rocks and stream ahead.

And in "The Vision," the speaker, driving back home from having dropped his wife at a station, encounters a hurt deer, an animal transfiguring into a

>   dim shape already
> half loving this fawn I saw and half
> something other, something in its mauled
> beauty I cannot find a name for.

Vocabulary of rocks and stream? Beauty he cannot find a name for? There it is, that link again. This time, instead of God (at least overtly), it's nature and art—the poet's, language. Art is physical; it's of the rocks and trees and water. So it's true, there is no choice. But that alone points up its mystery, that "something other" that is more than simply choice.

This isn't yet an answer, but it makes totemic the impulse. Words are the wafers and the wine. Whether you kneel at the altar rail or not, whether you choose or not (actively, that is; consciously), the wafer and the wine are wafer and wine. That doesn't change. They are of nature. Look again at the first four poems: "The Simple Truth About Snow" (water); "Building a Fire"; "Casting at Night" (air, water); "The Vision" (earth). Now go back to "The Simple Truth About Snow": "Christ, it seems I can't live/ clear of it," the speaker says. We know the referent of "it" is snow. Grammatically that's clear. And yet, ungrammatical though it is, we can't help seeing "Christ" as an equally valid referent. And sure enough, in the next verse section we find Hoey saying the white of snow "lancing" (nailing?) his eyes is "as white as God." And later he first compares himself, in his blindness, to Saul, and pledges that he'll "consecrate" his life, then, calmed by liquor, turns Indian-giver, asking, "What god holds a desperate soul/ to panicked vows?"

So he can't live clear of it. Extend the referent again: "it" means, of course, the snow, but also means the liquid fire of art, and that of God. As for those "panicked vows," well, "What god" hasn't been established yet. That lies ahead, if at all. But art? That's different. Panicked or not, those vows persist. And Hoey meets them with poem after poem, and in doing so moves us inexorably toward the three words that end his book: "...and I answer." However we interpret that answer, it is, essentially, an apotheosis. It is the taking of the wafer and the wine. That happens in (on) "The Bus to Common Center," one of the most important poems in the book.

In this poem the speaker, out for a walk one night, recalls another night and another walk with a friend during which he tells his friend about yet another night and his encounter with a bus in fog—a bus whose destination was Common Center. A night within a night within a night. A perfectly complex dramatic frame for a poem that turns to God and suffering and this benighted world and praise—above all, praise, at the end "calling to praise this fine day." It isn't far into the poem when we see clearly that the speaker's walk has become a symbol of a deeper journey, both inner and outer, both of this world and not; not far when we see that the bus is something more, appearing "through the fog" those nights "when you most need the ride," and taking you

> to some common center
> of suffering, a spot where all the weary
> souls might gather and share their pain to a common cure.

This bus is an express straight to the heart of things. Along the way, the speaker tells us about the walk shared with his friend, "our talk turned to God." For the friend, "the Holy Ghost/ which descends in a flutter of wings and leaves...its mark adorning the forehead" is everything. But for the speaker, himself "no Christian," God is something else entirely,

> For the Spirit, when it descends
>
> and leaves its holy fire, leaves a different fire
> for each of us, causing each of us
> to speak a different tongue of praise, perhaps
> to see different gods, while the Son
> makes us one, his love another bus to Common Center,
> for the Son is God infused in man, divinity
>
> driven through the genetic code, through
> and through to the common center
> of what, despite our uniqueness, makes us
> uniquely human, animal suffused with the spark of God,
> the clear
> light pouring down in hard brilliance like stars, the whole
> weight of mortality unknown to fire, the fading glow
>
> of foxfire on the brow.

There it is, in the rush and tumble of the words riding the lines like runaway toboggans spilling across the stanzas; there it is, in the music of the syntax, in the rhetoric of God and genes—there it is, the answer the whole book has been moving toward. For Hoey, God is "the love that endures/ into sunlight"; love "deeper/ than light ever shines" that, in the bones and flesh of his young son, his "left-handed bus/ to the day's common center," calls him

> back to the clear light
> lading the locust, the harvest of smells in the grass,
> calling to praise this fine day…

And he answers. There it is: God, Nature, and in the poetry of its expression—in, that is, the beauty of the words and form that is the poem—art. That trinity.

So in this poem of praise we leave the speaker kneeling at the altar. Not surprisingly, however, it's the getting to the altar that so moves us and convinces us his final answer is correct. That journey is the art that is the poem.

"The love that endures into sunlight" underscores again how central nature is to Hoey's vision. Nature is the center ring. All supervised by the ringmaster, whose voice changes costume as the need arises, in it gather the acrobats, the clowns, the trainers and, of course, the animals. There are a lot of animals in *A Fire in the Cold House of Being*; animals that, according to "this baldhead, this old fool" in "Listening for Bear," one of three major poems in the first section, "ain't likely to forget, nor/ I figure to forgive us for the land/ we took and leveled, blasted/ clear of trees and parceled-out/ with wire, rock and hedgerow." There are birds, deer, fish, bears, coyotes, rabbits, and, most memorable and shocking, a tapeworm. We encounter this stand-in symbol for the snake in "Sunday Rock" (along with "Listening for Bear" and "Fishing the Hudson"), one of the most successful and certainly most powerful poems in the book:

> I've been practicing medicine up here now
> for nearly fifty years, and I've seen it all.
> You're a poet, you must know Frost's 'Out, Out—.'
> I've seen so many severed fingers, toes,
> feet, arms, and legs, lost from sheer stupidity,
> I've lost count. Not to mention those mangled
> by tractors, balers, even milkers. Skulls

fractured by careless handling of cows,
and episodes with cows I shan't repeat.
Most of my practice seems to stem from love,
or the lack of it. Monday mornings, you must hear
the radio report the weekend body count.
Shootings and stabbings in bars, the worst in homes.
I got a call Sunday week, in the morning,
early. Man came home drunk, fit to beat his wife,
she beat him to it. Collapsed his lung and near
blew off his privates with a .22.

And incest. If I had to say, I guess
I'd say that's worst. The absolute damage.
Four, sometimes five years old.
                        They're not evil,
I don't guess, just living so long beyond
the reach of what we'd consider civilized...
I don't know. Sometimes I think the story's true.
There's a rock by the road a few miles north
of Tupper, you've maybe passed it, they call it
'Sunday Rock.' It marks, they claim, where you pass
north of the Adirondacks. Legend holds
that past that rock, even Sundays, the land
goes Godless. God's country, they might call it—
if so, God must spend his weekends in the city.
A spinster I used to call on—as a doctor—
lived out in the sticks. Pyrites. She'd phone
every other week, this complaint or that.
She had no family, never married. Lived
alone the fifteen years since her mother'd died.
Living alone like that does funny things
to a body's mind. I'd stop in, of course,
when I was out that way, each time she'd call.
Never much wrong. Just loneliness, and we
haven't yet found a cure for that.
                            Last year,

the calls suddenly stopped. When I hadn't heard
from her a good month, I dropped by. When I'd
about given up knocking, a soft shuffling
came inside, the curtains parted. Knocked again,
and she finally answered.
          The door just cracked
and she peered out, nervous, a way I'd never
seen her. After a word, she let me in.
I stepped inside and she began to cry.
'I knew someone would find me out,' she said.
'I thought it'd be the reverend, though, not you.'
She wouldn't quiet—broke from me when I tried
to sit her down and calm her. Walked from door
to window, back to door, her hands wringing
each other.
          I wondered if she'd had a stroke,
but when I questioned her, she brought a small
oak box, coffin-shaped, down from the highboy
and thrust it in my hands. 'I don't know when,'
she cried, 'I don't know how—the Devil took me
for his mistress. I bore him out a child,'
she wept, 'a serpent. I bore it out and
killed it!' When I opened the box, inside,
on pure white satin, lay the longest tapeworm
I have ever seen. Head flattened by a poker.

Significantly, "Sunday Rock," like the others (though "Fishing the Hudson" doesn't have a "you" established really), is a dramatic monolog; significant because it points up one of Hoey's accomplishments: his ability to create masks. In monologs the mask is voice, and Hoey clearly has mastered both the language and the tone such voice demands, especially that of rural folk. Both "Sunday Rock" and "Listening for Bear" are monologs belonging to the Frostian tradition—two of the finest I know of (some others being those of Hayden Carruth's). In "Listening for Bear," the longer of the two, the speaker, an "old fool," recounts an encounter with what might have been a bear, seeing it as an omen of our ecological comeuppance, and along the way tells us much of whom he is: an erstwhile farmer, paper mill employee now retired, a widower. His language is that special mix of the rural colloquial and the poetry of the natural world in which he's spent his life. He's shrewd in his knowledge, wise in his patience, and humble in his vision. Not surprisingly, his talk is peppered with references to the Bible, and to the Lord who, he's convinced, "sent before a bear to do his bidding." His God is the one straight out of the Old Testament, the God who, "when he gets mad… don't know a golden rule." This is the God before whose terrible instrument, the bear, he stands "stiller than in prayer." Like Faulkner's bear, this one embodies a primeval truth. So does the tapeworm in "Sunday Rock."

Nature might be the center ring in Hoey's poems, the voices central characters, but God is never very far away. That's especially true in this poem, which is, essentially, a morality play set on the vast stage of the Adirondacks, in a place where

> even Sundays, the land
> goes Godless. God's country, they might call it—
> if so, God must spend his weekends in the city.

It's a place where, amid the human carnage of the spirit and the flesh, God, if He's there, keeps hidden in the dark and terrifying thickets of the human heart, leaving the people living there, although "not evil," to their own devices, and those of the Devil:

> Monday mornings, you must hear
> the radio report the weekend body count.

Set down in the isolation of this Godless land, alone and lost, like all the "severed fingers, toes/ feet, arms, and legs," to "sheer stupidity," these are the Chosen people led into the desert and abandoned to their superstitions, remnants of old-time belief in an old God, that of the Old Testament: wrathful, but for them the ultimate dropout. The comic devastation of the spinster points this up. As told by the country doctor, the by turns compassionate and angry speaker of the poem, she had lived "alone the fifteen years since her mother'd died," and "Living alone like that does funny things/ to a body's mind." What it has done to hers is comic pathos at its best:

> 'I don't know when,'
> she cried, 'I don't know how—the Devil took me
> for his mistress. I bore him out a child,'
> she wept, 'a serpent. I bore it out and
> killed it.'

It, laid out on white satin in a "small oak box, coffin-shaped," was "the longest tapeworm" the doctor had ever seen. If, in "God, While Creating the Birds, Sees Adam in His Thoughts," Hoey wondered

> how God,
> creating first His angels, could have said
> the birds in gorgeous flight,
>
> then molded us from dust, flexed
> our bones, and finally left the feathers
> off,

in "Sunday Rock" the country doctor makes it clear there is no "making ourselves angels." There is only sin, suffering, guilt, and the grotesque atonement that is the inheritance left sad souls like the widow by a God who spends "his weekends in the city." Ironically enough, the doctor says it best: "Most of my practice seems to stem from love,/ or the lack of it." In another, smaller lyric, Hoey says of the character it describes,

> There's no
>
> such thing, he read someplace, as true black,
> only darkened blues.

In "Sunday Rock," a monolog that owes so much to Frost, the black is all too true.

God's never very far away. Sometimes, however, absence is His presence. This surely is true in "Fishing the Hudson"; in its violence of language and image, and most certainly in the gathering symphony of its music, it's the most powerful single poem in the book. Here the overwhelming power of the starkly dramatic circumstance has fused perfectly with the equally powerful language it requires.

(Kingston Point, New York)

On those spring days when dinner was done, darkness claiming
just a little less of evening every passing day,
I'd pedal down past swampland slowly shedding winter's drabness,
through the rusted hulks of oil tanks to the piers.
      I tried
casting with the same practiced snap of wrist and forearm
I'd watched my father use, plunking minnows halfway across a creek
as accurate as bullets. Tried to make my child's muscles
master all that grace and distance, but somehow, minutes later
my red cork bobber cowered near the pilings.
      The line
plumbed foaming oil scum, skin of weeds, peels, and roe,
unfurled to lure whatever from their lairs of mud and
        stone.
I knew, even on the best of nights, the best I'd catch
was sunnies, or too-small perch, or crappies, or bullhead
suckered from the muck with worms. Each night I'd gut them,
at twilight bike them home and sneak them in the freezer;
each night my mother threw them out.
      Still, we fished,
a few friends and I, almost every night we dipped our
        lines
and eyed the gang of black kids settled down the jetty,
daubing handlines, drinking beers, and smoking, smirking
        back.

We managed our uneasy truce; we, more anxious
not to linger into dark, would mount our bikes and leave
in groups of four or five, nervous for the stragglers,
but nervous
more each one for himself, each one scared of facing up to black,
whatever form he found it in.
                      One evening I'd caught nothing,
snagged rocks and wasted precious line, two or three snelled hooks,
and twice as many worms. The sun dipped lower, and all
my friends pulled in and pedaled home. The sun dipped lower,
light channeled through the huge rusting drums behind me,
struck a patch of unpeeled silver paint and made it
bleed, hemorrhage like a cracked egg of whatever unknown creatures
those pilings were the legs of—I thought of them that
                                    way,
dinosaurs built upside down, frayed legs of monsters
buried in the bottom muck, those thick legs
all that showed of some creature sleeping for a thousand years
that might wake one night we tossed our lines inside
its sleeping belly.
                I never told my friends about the
                           legs,
afraid they'd call me crazy, laugh and back away—half
to poke fun, half because they meant it.
                              The bobber trembled,
jerked me free of dreaming: buoyed frozen while I took
the slack, twitched again, then plummeted from sight,
line taut, thrumming like a high-tension wire.
I grasped the rod, afraid to touch the hissing handles,
watching nylon whine off the reel, shooting straight for bottom
black. No bullhead ever put up such a fight,
pulling like a thing possessed; no carp, no rock bass, nothing
ever bent the rod so nearly double: I prayed
my tackle—ancient springs and rusty screws—could endure,
prayed it wouldn't take into the pilings, scribbling
line in cyphers around those mammoth legs, snap the line

and vanish, my bobber trailing like a banner.
                         I reeled wildly,
unable to imagine what creature strained my line, trying
                         all
my muscles just to play it in. It fought me
every yard, every dripping inch of line: I felt once or
                         twice
my sneakers start to slide, could feel the pier begin to fall away
above me as it tugged: I clung fiercely to my reel
as it hauled me, hauled me down and under, down
where it was always black, blacker there than night,
where light would never find me.
                         I watched it
break surface. Its heaving snake-shape soaped oil slick
in its frenzy, snarling yards of line before I fought it
to the planking, dragged its ugly arm-length onto
                         concrete,
writhing loops of nylon into a maze even my great-aunt's fingers
would not be able to divine.
                         Some black kids wandered over
to watch me reckon with the eel, too mindful of my feet,
so small beside its jaws, to worry at their closeness.
'Take this stick,' one of them called over, 'you got to
take this stick and beat that sucker bloody, beat that
                         devil
dead before it bite you. Not too close, mind—else them
                         jaws,
they take you, they grab your hand, and once they on you,
boy, ain't nothing on this earth can free you, less you
take a knife and cut that hand away!' He spat to one side,
shook his head and watched me worry with the reel.
                         I took
his stick and struck its head: snake-jaws
seized the stick and wouldn't loosen though I tried
to kick it free. I took a rock and bashed it; watched
                         blood

appear and bashed again, finally cut the line as close
to those stuck jaws its boiling tail allowed. I held that stick
at arm's length and swung it high, saw it hang there
for an instant, snake-shape fluming like a pennant, before I tore it
down to concrete, shattered flesh and fish-skull, casting up and down,
its blood flecked, flung around the pier with bits of bone and mucus.
'Fucker!' I yelled, 'bastard-mother-sonofabitch!'—I sang
those words I'd heard my father use, used them then
the way my great-aunt used her hymnal: 'Jesus-Christ-GodDAMN!'

When its teeth released I flailed the carcass, striking
at its eyes, its jaws, its gills, striking again and
        again.
The black boys backed away. 'Boy,' they laughed,
'you're crazy!'
    I pushed the dead thing toward the water;
with a final swing I sent it spinning, red blood and grey scales
down between the pilings. I tossed the bloody stick
in after. What little line I could, I wound back slowly;
gathered all the rest into a damp nest that held my
        bobber.
I dumped my mix of coffee grounds and dirt, the few
remaining worms, and dipped a bit of water from a puddle.
Three tins I used, scrubbing blood from concrete with my sneaker,
before I scooped my worms up, lashed my rod
fast to a fender and pedaled into night.

"Fishing the Hudson," on the surface, is about a boy's initiation into a self-knowledge that is dark and violent. Turned around, that knowledge is the dark and violence—in him, whether his savage killing of an eel he catches, or the primal fear he feels at being the only white among the "gang of black kids" on the jetty. The racial fear is kept below the surface, but it percolates, layering the poem with its black film, and thereby piling on more fuel until the boy erupts in the climactic scene. But really, what this poem is all about is evil. "Fishing the Hudson" is a mini-*Moby Dick*. The eel he beats to death is the boy's white whale;

the boy is Ishmael and Ahab both: Ishmael because he wins, Ahab because he loses. He wins in that he, too, survives, tells his tale, and gives the moral, which is the knowledge of the self he's gained. He loses in the getting of the knowledge, in the knowledge he receives, and in the knowledge he must take away as, in the end, he gathered his bait, lashed his rod, and "pedaled into night." Even his deckhands, those black kids, sense what's at stake. Coming over to watch the epic struggle, one of them says,

> you got to
> take this stick and beat that sucker bloody, beat that
> devil
> dead before it bite you. Not too close, mind—else them
> jaws,
> they take you, they grab your hand, and once they on you,
> boy, ain't nothing on this earth can free you, less you
> take a knife and cut that hand away!

Literally, yes. He could cut his hand away. But metaphorically, no. There is no cutting away that night he pedals into at the end. Once you have knowledge, you have it. Madness, or obsession with icons, is the price of freedom from yourself—like, for example, the widow in "Sunday Rock." In that poem, the widow, pathetically, by clinging to her God, is herself abandoned. Atonement has its cost. In "Fishing the Hudson" the reverse is true:

> 'Fucker!' I yelled, 'bastard-mother-sonofabitch!'—I sang
> those words I'd heard my father use, used them then
> the way my great-aunt used her hymnal:
> 'Jesus-Christ-GodDAMN!'

The yoking of obscenity, that most violent of languages, with the divine, here used also as obscenity, tells it all. Here it's God who is abandoned:

> I clung fiercely to my reel
> as it hauled me, hauled me down and under, down
> where it was always black, blacker there than night,
> where light would never find me.

And by the end light hasn't found him. For the boy's aunt, using her hymnal like, no doubt, a sword or shield, God's never far away. But for the boy, after his terrible initiation on the pier, he is.

On an immediate, visceral level, then, "Fishing the Hudson" is a wrenching poem. While "Sunday Rock" also has at its center the darkness of the world, its rendering is very different. The doctor, in relating to us the drama of the widow and her tapeworm, keeps it at a safe remove; it is a scene set on a stage. It's somehow make-believe, its terrible absurdity at best a shocking verisimilitude. But in "Fishing the Hudson" something more occurs. The incident the boy recounts is of the past, but in the telling it becomes not-past, becomes an epic action spilling from the stage and pulling in the audience, making it part of the action. Formal barriers, that is, are swept away. Other than that inherent in the event itself, the power of this poem, and its real triumph, is its language and its technical proficiency. Look at the lines, many of which go thirteen syllables or more, how they take us out in great swoops, like a tide, then rush back in from the horizon through enjambment, tentacles of liquid syllables, explosive vowels, alliterated consonants, line breaks and caesurae set like buoys in a stormy sea.

There is no sectioning really; the only spatial break occurs near the end of the poem, appropriately right after the boy's explosive "Jesus-Christ-GodDAMN!" Instead, by dropping the start of a new sentence one space down, usually at the end of a line, Hoey achieves the effect of sectioning without actually breaking the poem into stanzas, thus allowing him to avoid any disjunction of the rhetoric, which builds and builds into a lava-heated, oceanic swell of words. It's Whitman, of course, but without the excess. Language shrewdly and most exactingly used both super-heats the rhetoric and the rhythm, and at the same time acts as a natural check. Rhetorical patterns always argue logic; logic, control. Notice, for instance, how the language gathers force through careful pacing: how the subtle implications of the "darkness claiming" changes later to the group of boys scared of "facing up to black"; how the language and imagery get progressively militant as the tension mounts—the boy remembering how his father plunked "minnows halfway across a creek as accurate as bullets"; the boy describing how his "red cork bobber cowered near the pilings," the bullhead "suckered from the muck," the "uneasy truce," the rusting drums the sun makes "bleed, hemorrhage like a cracked egg," the "hissing handles, nylon whine of the reel, shooting straight for/ bottom black." Even the Anglo-Saxon-like epithets add to the mood of violence of the primeval scene: "snake-shape," "snake-jaws." And as in *Beowulf*, there's a mixture of the pagan and the Christian. The boy imagines the jetty with its pilings as

> dinosaurs built upside down, frayed legs of monsters
> buried in the bottom muck, those thick legs
> all that showed of some creature sleeping for a thousand years
> that might wake one night we tossed our lines inside
> its sleeping belly.

There's Grendel, and there's Jonah's whale, that "sleeping belly" from which, unlike Jonah, no boy, once swallowed, will escape. Leviathan, the fearful symbol of God's wrath. And after God, what's left? His wrath, that's all. Hoey underscores this a few lines earlier in the poem with juxtaposition. He has the boy recount his nervousness, and his friends', as being

> more each one for himself, each one scared of facing up to black,
> whatever form he found it in,

then drops one space and says, "One evening I'd caught nothing." Nothing. It echoes in your ears like one of those rusted drums on the pier. The play is obvious yet doesn't make you smile. And look at the very end. The boy, "with a final swing," sends the dead eel "spinning, red blood and/ grey scales/ down between the pilings," then "tossed the bloodied stick in after." He could be Cain discarding the weapon he used to kill his brother, Abel. Of course, symbolically that's exactly what he's done. And then there is the dark, the way it grows throughout the poem, through both direct references and, generally, the thrust of the imagery. Again, at the beginning the dark is "claiming just a little less," but by the end, like the first parents, he's cast out, and takes his "solitary way," pedaling into night. So much for Eden. So much for the God of the first parents, that of his aunt. Separated, as the poem makes clear, from his father by his failure to "master all that grace and distance" fishing, and from his mother when the fish he'd gutted and sneaked into the freezer "each night" she "threw... out," he now is separated from the icons of belief—from God. His innocence invalidated, and in a place "where even light would never find" him, the boy, having fought the eel and dragged it onto concrete, watches as it thrashes

> writhing loops of nylon into a maze even my great-aunt's fingers
> would not be able to divine.

Divine. How that word refuses to be stopped by its period. How its irony travels into silence, like a string of echoes dissipating into nothing. How the echoes make coarse the tongue, like ash.

There are other poems in Hoey's book that, like the ones discussed, are major efforts: "Hymns to a Tree," "The Left-Handed Marriage" and "Toil," a sonnet crown for his father. As the opening sonnet alone illustrates, "Toil" illustrates the author's mastery of even the most traditional of forms. And even here, where the formal and the technical demands are exact, Hoey never allows them to subsume his natural tone of voice:

> Where I grew up men's hands were not stained brown
> digging potatoes, reaping wheat or corn
> or spading peat from bogs to keep them warm.
> Bricked dust rouged skin raw; the cement plant ground
> a fine grey silt in skin, which fell around
> a couple miles on houses, too. What form
> their corn and barley took was bottled, more
> to cut the taste of grime at first then pound
> the work from mind. When he got home, he toiled,

after he shed his working clothes—as though
that dirt might somehow blight the cleaner soil—
in his small garden. My father turned his hand
to peas and squash, but most he loved tomatoes:
their taste a work his tongue could understand.

The voice is simple, down to earth, straightforward. It's a most plain opening for a sonnet, resisting the histrionics of a dazzling line or image. This is a human being speaking, not a "character." This seems to be generally true of Hoey's first-person poems, and is attractive for its honesty and its intimacy. This is a real-life person. But, as always, God is never very far away:

Their taste a work my tongue could understand,
I thought: transforming bread to body, wine
to Christ's bright blood inside.

And neither is language, the

                                          bland bread
become as honeyed baklava unfolded
on tongue then liquored with a holy mead
of song. Broad vowels and breaded consonants...

"Toil" is a poem about work ethics, father/son relationships, and language.

                                   Most days I lean, all hot
and bothered by a misplaced comma, 'we'
misused for 'us,'

the speaker says, but knows enough to add,

                                   My pen's no plough, red
ink not my life's blood to spill on essays

concerning drinking age and draft or gun
control or silly pets.

For, though his wife, giving birth, has "scribed" her work "in joy," he knows full well "We are not gardeners, though/ the metaphor is tempting." In this recognition that the tenor and the vehicle are not of equal truth and therefore weight, the speaker does real honor to the language and himself. Properly, art should heighten life, not take its place—as if it could. No, Hoey's after more important things. He'd will, he says, his son

> more balance in his life, more light, the grace
> to face each morning's darkness without dread.

And in "What We Hold To," a poem in which he wonders what his son will hold to, he admits,

> Between us, words, like nails in seasoned wood,
> drive slow through toughened grain,

but in "The Word" he tells his son

> *There is a word,*
> ... for this harsh song,
> one song heard—as we step
> outside—among many this day
> bright as May in early March.
> Listen—we will find it.

We will find it. There is hope, determination, whimsy and a slight romanticism in these words. And certainly, the counterpoint is always there. "Song isn't enough," Hoey states baldly in "The Left-Handed Marriage," a poem which, in its achingly beautiful lyricism, declares implicitly that the word has been found. And, as in the beginning, it's the word made flesh:

> We cheat death
> with children, our never-ending
> engendering spirals. Cast them
> out into time with our faith they
> will outlast us, songs of our love
> made meat.

Language, like God, is rooted in the natural. The house of being might be cold, but it contains the kindling and the fire. Admittedly, Orpheus, whom the speaker thinks Orion "might be better named," was not successful, and

> With no
> child to comfort him, who could blame
> Orpheus for trying to cheat
> death, trying with only his song
> to drag love together?

But, just as "Faith assures each night I will rise/ again from the marriage bed" and "walk out into the night," so, too, does faith assure the song's continuation. And song is what this is. In its five sections "The Left-Handed Marriage" gives us Hoey at his lyric best. It has the hushed, intense, exclusive timbre of Kinnell in some of his more personal poems—like, say, "After Making Love We Hear Footsteps." Its evocation of the sexual is close, much like the air before a storm, but never lapses into cheap cliches. And, too, the language always keeps its music, even at its most abstract, which in this poem is grounded in the lyricism and therefore works:

> for who can doubt, with the explosive
> sighing of climax, the fierce thrashing
> of loins, that more than seed
> is give, that we give up, we give
> into each other from both ends at once,
> giving of spirit, of essence, loosing each night
> a little the love that holds us, yet not
> losing but using it to bind us, for that moment...

"Explosive sighing"? "Climax"? "Spirit"? "Essence"? Though the subject here is sex, these words could as easily apply to language. Abstract, yes. But look at what results: pure music—all those participles, line enjambments, rush and tumble syntax. Here the talk, the urge to lecture, to be abstract, is contained and made effective by the sound, the music born of careful word choice and syntax, both characteristic of Hoey's work.

Another poem, the sectional "Hymns to a Tree," is directly concerned with the abstract. But unlike far too many poems in lesser hands, Hoey avoids the always clear and present problems of awkward rhetoric, unconvincing voice and overweening polemics. To the contrary, "Hymns to a Tree" achieves two goals Hoey struggles toward throughout his book: naming and praising. Rilke's Angel is always looking over his shoulder, certainly in this poem. And so is God. This is evident, first, in the poem's title and, second, in the section titles: "Tree-of Heaven," "Passion," "The Nature of Soul," "Aevum," "Pentecostal" and "Harvest." The tree, an ailanthus, is addressed directly, and becomes a leafy Jesus Christ, the drama of his promise, passion, resurrection and transfiguration enacted by and metamorphosed into the tree:

> What comes on the wind is more than air.
> God's voice plays in the green flame of your leaves,
> the silent music of all nature brought to flower in your
>   burning,
> a burning that leaves all it touches
> whole: purified, sanctified, for the first time
> completely one of soul and body...

Nature and God, God and Nature. There it is again. Perhaps more directly than in any poem in the book, and certainly more elaborately, in "Hymns to a Tree" Hoey's mix of Christian iconography and pantheism blend into a complex and compelling art. This time the intimacy is real because it's both physical and of the mind and spirit, in both the dramatic context and in the language. Consider the last section of "Harvest":

> Now in mid-autumn, this first leaf-fall
> in a new house, the red maple
> stolid in the yard has dropped its bright
> leaves on the lawn. And you call me,
> across the cold distance, this night
> of the first killing frost, rime heavy
> on air, you call me to harvest.
> What fruit? Not apple nor pear; your leaves
> have ripened through green to a dazzling
> orange flame and now dangle, the ash
> of your glory. What fruit? The cardinals or squirrels?
> This invisible fruit you bear me
> across cold distance, tasteless, unfolds
> itself on the air—cold fire, apple virtue:
> the shape of you bright on my tongue.

Things of this world, meet metaphor. And notice, too, the tree's "shape" is "bright on his *tongue*" (italics mine). There it is: language again. Nature, God and language. In section three, "The Nature of Soul," the speaker says:

> You say, in a voice
> some might say I heard
> only from deep within me,
>
> in language, as some
> have likewise said, you
> you cannot possibly know
>
> you know me, you tell me:
> the delicate tips
> from the twig's end taste air, fold
>
> slowly open from
> a space within, this
> green heart, this speed unfolding.

It's lovely in its delicate lyricism and graceful in its form. The language the speaker hears is both real and that which is deeper and actually beyond the phonemes of mere words; it's physical and more than physical, as only the language of "God" could be. This section illustrates as well as any why the rhetoric in this poem works so well. The *idea* of the verse, and the language, meld themselves into a unity. The wordplay, the abstraction and the imagery are integrated perfectly; they are like the tree: heartwood and bark.

This integration never fails, precisely because the language never does. This is evident from the first section on. In "Tree-of-Heaven" we are introduced to the ailanthus, the roots of which are "imperiling/ the house's foundation," and of which the speaker is protector, having "kept them from you," the ones who call it "trash tree" and would fell it. The tree, much like the one Frost talks about in "Tree at my Window," is outside the window, "rooted in earth" yet "spreading, less constrained by air, upward," going "both ways beyond the pane." The language, furthered by the syntax and the enjambment of the tercets, is, in its fine blend of the abstract idea and the concrete details, Hoey at his rhetorical best. Among other things, he can move a complex syntax—all those repetitions and participles—forward into lyric beauty with the best of poets; and when he says to the ailanthus, its "heights rivaling an oak's" and in the wind its "supple length" dancing, that

>   celebrating air
> as no oak ever, a sermon wrought more subtly than stone,
> your greater spread draws me both ways I lack at once,

We believe him and respond both to the lyricism of the language and the intimacy of his voice—precisely because the sermon *is* wrought more subtly. And in "Passion," the second section, with its yoking of the tree and Christ, we believe him when he says that, no matter "how you must suffer, rooted/ in this unseasonable cold," you

> have watched this hour long the sky
> brighten, the sun's light—

> before the sun ever shines, gleams
> as this moment it promises,
> above rooftops—glowingly
> descend the length of you.

We believe in the cleansing fire of suffering. Likewise, in "Aevum" we believe when he says that, even though beset in his thinking by the "terrible Angel of the Stillness," the cold night is "in your presence gone/ suddenly summer," and that "Only *you*, you bend your boughs down,/ uppermost down to embrace me." We believe him because the whole poem is a prayer for metamorphosis, the tree and speaker come together, joined as tree and man, Man-Tree:

> for it is the incandescence of essence burning,
> the light of God converting sap to soul,
> the combustion, the conflagration of all nature in you,
> a single candled tree.

Call the tree ailanthus, or call it God. Either way, the language makes the difference. The language is the tongue that shapes the metamorphosis and, in the shaping, is the "silent music of all nature brought to flower," is the fire that martyrs the cold house of being.

Fire is always an ambiguous symbol. Fire creates, and fire destroys. Fire is Prometheus chained to his rock and all too human in his pride and in his courage; fire is Zeus, the smithy of Creation, punisher of man's transgressions. Fire is sin, and fire is the purgation of sin. There's all of this, and, in *A Fire in the Cold House of Being*, there's the fire that rages on the poet's tongue: There's language. And, among other things, Hoey's graceful "The Things of August" is, most importantly, about language—or rather, the limits of language faced with all the beauty of even the things of this world, let alone the spiritual.

Clearly, if "Sunday Rock" is the most gothic of the poems and "Fishing the Hudson" the most powerful and "Toil" the most moving, "The Things of August" is the most elegant:

"Preise dem Engel die Welt..." —Rilke

Already autumn tinges the air, bruising
my senses still tuned to summer: the sudden
gusts, the sun here and gone again
all day, and the peculiar scent, faintly
acrid with ozone, autumn rain
has all of its own in the dry rustling of leaves
too soon brightening toward fall. I would number

the sights of August if I thought such praise
could somehow resurrect a single day
of mid-summer or likewise lengthen summer
even a day—the first I have felt such
regret since when as a child fall meant not so much
school again as the end of time
devoted purely to play. But doesn't Rilke say

we shouldn't try to tell the angel
our splendid sensations! Rather we should
praise the world: tell him the Things and he'll stand
the more astonished at the flux of time,
the flow of seasons, and the way we
so surely, in hand and eye, make things
a part of ourselves. I could name
the many flowers seen by the roadside: gentian
and aster, lupine and once pearly
Queen Anne's lace now tightly curled,
wild chicory and daisies, sow-thistle candelabra,
bright flares of sumac, and tiger lily torches
lighting the last days of summer; and birds,

the least fraction of which I
can name: sparrows and robins and starlings
most plentifully, an abundance of pigeons and crows,
house finches, bluejays, and cardinals, bright guests,

an occasional chickadee glimpsed
deep in leafage, a ghostly floating
owl at dusk, but most and nearest

my heart the undulating shimmer
of goldfinches brightening the roadside bloom;
this last day of a darkening month a whole
hillside, where most often they flash
in solitary flight or two in bobbing harmony,
erupted their glory, a full symphony,
a plenum of birds, to mark
summer's end. But what are these

but things? Can numbering the things
I've witnessed be enough? And what of wonder?
Can I trust the Angel to know,
as men—myself not least among them, not knowing
what to call by half these things
beheld, as though naming could in all possibility
adequately praise what I see—
so often forget, it is not
in the fact but in the way of seeing that miracles
arise. In the advent

of fall, the scales, on a day such as this,
fully dropped from my eyes, the manifold
things of this world not yet completely
given over to spirit shine more surely, more
manifestly themselves than ever before,
this final bloom before they yield in one last
explosion of color to the pure serenity

of deep winter, enthralled by clarities of frost:
the whole momentum of summer
gathered to this day, a metamorphosis
no less splendid for its constant

> re-enactment, when leaf, petal, and feather,
> a concert of color, burn
> in a single day's turning to spirit.
>
> What Angel presides at this turning?
> And how, the sight of a hillside gone
> suddenly gold still brightening
> my eyes, shall I praise it?

It's a wonderful rumination on the change of seasons, beauty, naming things, Rilke, and miracles, which are not "in the fact but in the way of seeing." It's a poem of birds and flowers and colors and, rendered as they are in lovely language, music. Of the birds, for instance, Hoey writes about the "ghostly floating/ owl at dusk," then tells us that "most and nearest" his heart is the "undulating shimmer of goldfinches," those birds most beloved by Mandelstam. It's a poem, in short, of language and nature and God, and, more than any other poem in the collection, poses the fundamental question for the poet: How, in a world so much divorced from God and nature and language—certainly that of poetry—how can the poet praise?

"The Things of August" opens with the autumn "bruising" the speaker's "senses still tuned to summer" with its sights and smells. He is moved and would, he says,

>   number
> the sights of August if I thought such praise
> could somehow resurrect a single day
> of mid-summer or likewise lengthen summer
> even a day...

He would, but

>   doesn't Rilke say
> we shouldn't try to tell the Angel
> our splendid sensations? Rather we should

> praise the world: tell him the Things and he'll stand
> the more astonished at the flux of time,
> the flow of seasons, and the way we
> so surely, in hand and eye, make things
> a part of ourselves.

It's a lovely passage, and, in emphasizing world over self, "Things" over "sensations," it takes us further even than William Carlos Williams and his "no ideas but in things." Here we're involved with aesthetics, even the spiritual. Ironically, it's precisely the senses, downplayed here, that will be necessary to the praise. We can't praise what we can't partake of, and making things "a part of ourselves" is the ultimate praise. The rest is art. The rest is language. But is "naming" enough? He could, the speaker says, name roadside flowers, which he proceeds to do in one stanza, and birds, also in one stanza, echoing the traditional pastoral epithalamium, with its extended catalogs. "But what," he wonders, "are these/ but things?" and "Can numbering the things/ I've witnessed be enough?" This question is rhetorical. It's the next that states the speaker's real concern: "And what of wonder?" If men themselves so often forget that "it is not in the fact but in the way of seeing that miracles/ arise," can the Angel know? One way men see, of course, is through language. And what lovely language comprises the next two stanzas—textbook examples of how abstraction can be rendered into the poetic. All the "scales" dropped from his eyes, the speaker sees just how

>   the manifold
> things of this world not yet completely
> given over to spirit shine more surely, more
> manifestly themselves than ever before,
> this final bloom before they yield in one last
> explosion of color to the pure serenity
>
> of deep winter, enthralled by clarities of frost...

The passage, in its evocation of a "metamorphosis," a "splendid enactment" of a moment caught spectacularly on the very edge of its seasonal obliteration, calls to mind Wallace Stevens' dictum: "Death is the mother of beauty." Nature, "in a single day's turning to spirit," yields, as Hoey puts in in "Fire in the Trees," a wonderful lyric prefacing "The Things of August," "essence to air." But the problem remains, even more so given such ephemeral moments of transfiguration, and the last stanza of this splendid poem returns us to the aesthetic, and spiritual, dilemma:

> What Angel presides at this turning?
> And how, the sight of a hillside gone
> suddenly gold still brightening
> my eyes, shall I praise it?

Again, if "Fishing the Hudson" is the most powerful poem in the book, "The Things of August" is the most elegant—a beautifully cohesive poem bringing together God, Nature and language, those three strands in Hoey's triple helix that is *A Fire in the Cold House of Being*. Wonderfully enough, he doesn't even mention God; yet God, in this poem more than any other, is a presence that is palpable—in the essential problem, both aesthetic and epistemological; in the absorption of Rilke; in the throbbing poetry. But even more amazingly, the poem answers its own question even as, ironically, it leaves the answer open. This, however, is not a clever evasion. First, it has been earned. Daring to ask the question, to stoke the fire in the cold house of being, and then, having followed each potential answer to its inevitable dead end, to finish with a clear-eyed acceptance of the question itself as answer is remarkable. More to the point, though, is that the poetry itself, the aching music with which Hoey has transfigured the things of this world, those "facts," sustains and guards against a lapse into the merely rational and clever. Strangely, for a poem that is evocative of Rilke, lush both in its details and its rhetoric, "The Things of August" is the most Greek of the poems in Hoey's book. It's speculative, metaphysical, deeply moral in its probing, eco-natural, personal in the most unself-conscious sense, and, like so many poems in this memorable book, damned fine sculpting, marble all the way. It's the poem in which Hoey is closest to the bone. Look, once more, at that last stanza:

What Angel presides at this turning?
And how, the sight of a hillside gone
suddenly gold still brightening
my eyes, shall I praise it?

That's poetry: all of the good earth, the good heavens, the Angel good in spite of its, and our, ambivalence, and all the good in us. That's poetry.

How, Allen Hoey asks, is he to praise it?—the Angel and the realm, the fire and the cold house of being.

The answer is clear. He already has.

The author, George Drew with poet Allen Hoey

Farewell

I Should Have Read the Greeks More Closely

In Memoriam,
Allen Hoey, 1952-2010

1. *From Autumn*

God, to write a poem like that!

Last night there were mists as thick as glop
old women use to mask their faces, but
rain was also flooding the roads
you drove with a friend, a new CD
humming—but not like bees—and your small
talk seeding the close and soggy air.
The wind blew hard. It wasn't mellow,
and fruit, such as it was, was something you
bought in that co-op you like so much.
Apples? Hazel shells? Hell, you don't know
how to tell zucchini from summer squash.

Well, that was yesterday. Tonight you walk
abroad with your close bosom-friend,
tired of your book-lined upstairs room,
drowsy from hours of work. It's true
the landscape's urban, but there's a moon,
and the smell of half-dead flowers sticking
to everything as you cut through the park
where aspens twitter and the brook gasps,
walk tree-lined residential streets and end
back at your house where you'll sit late
swatting life with words no bigger than gnats.

There is a garden of sorts, but back
of the garage, and even if there were

robins and crickets you'd never know,
not from inside. Lambs are pictures in books.
From the kitchen table, where you strip
the contacts from your eyes, you hear
your father working the zipper of his snores.
What difference Eden anyhow? Inside or out
it's the same: a little Heaven, a lot of Hell.
You tell your friend about the columbine
you saw. God, how the spiked heads drooped.

2. *Cussing Allen*

Mainers call them hicks not rednecks, he said.
And would, I asked, "cussing" be a hick or redneck term?
He wasn't sure, but he was that "Cussing Allen"
would be one helluva title for a poem.
But what would I cuss him for? I suppose
I could wreak revenge for his liberal use of red
on all the drafts I've sent him over the years,
or for the time he put, "by accident" in an Indian dish,
a pepper so hot it nearly incinerated my taste buds.
But cussing like that is lyric and brief,
not the epic the title he suggested cries out for.
So I declined, telling him he was just too sweet,
that like the long Latinate periodic sentences
he was so masterly at, such cussing was beyond my talent
and would be misplaced, to which he muttered, "You
dickhead! I meant it as an adjective." Well, I said,
cussing him under my breath for calling me that,
maybe I should title it Cussing George.

3. *I Should Have Read the Greeks More Closely*

Between goodbye and the email that was
supposed to greet me when I arrived
back home came the ringing of the phone,

my crisp hello and her husky voice:
Oh god, he's had another heart attack....
And to think, he was so happy, so
beguiled by poetry and our friendship,
so on fire with language rendered
in the style of the ancient Greeks. And me?
Likewise beguiled, by destiny's sweet embrace:
twenty-five years of friendship, hair
gone silver together, and oh the golden bough
on which we imagined ourselves installed
forever, poem after poem our battle call
rousing the dawn to another perfection,
the breaking of our branch unimaginable.
I should have read the Greeks more closely.

4. *On the Outskirts of Paradise*
                      "With friends like you,
                                  who needs angels?"

First there is the body, the sheer beautiful bulk
of blood, bones, ligaments and tendons, organs,
skin, succulent skin, the body wrapped in it,
body entwined with air, body with earth,
body grappling, all the large and little acts of love:
breaking wind, belching, braying at the world.
His mostly large, each a big bear hug: *Dickhead*,
his greeting; *Numbnuts*, mine. Or *Bubba*, his;
Boyo, mine. Snarling, snapping at the world,
wildly at odds with it, curses coming one
after another, each a four-letter feathered thug
breaking through hard bark, drilling all the way in
to a rotten core, gutting it. First was this body,
his body, the outsized girth and grace of it,
and now, in the end, there is this loss of body,
its grime, its sweet stench of love, this manly love,
its work of body, body of work, its easy obscenity.

5. *Getting My Hands Dirty*

Whatever he wasn't, he was a poet always,
ready for the poem to announce itself,
even in the dreamless depths of sleep;
and now he is the poem's dead language,
its declensions and conjugations on the tip
of no one's tongue. I'm a poet, too,
but my hands aren't yet dirty enough,
the script I apply illegible as pictures
drawn in dust and left to the designs
of rain and wind and the assault of time.
I lack it utterly, but if I had the courage,
I'd view him on the table, cold
stainless steel table, his body naked
beneath a plastic sheet. If I had it,
I'd touch his cheeks, his eyes, his ears, his lips;
inspect the bruises on his nose and chin,
markers of the moment he fell forward out
of time; I'd bend, my body pressed to his,
two men in a manly embrace, poet to poet;
and the poem, this poem, at last, ready for him.

6. *On the Way to Allen's Wake*

Tomorrow I'll ignore the ashes and to the embers
he kept glowing in his cold house of being raise
a toast; as best I can I'll effect a brogue bubbly
with Irish strut and destroy the dirty jokes he loved,
which today, driving south on the Taconic Parkway,
I'm trying to recall. It's a beautiful day,
and hawks are everywhere plying their craft,
their wing tips inscribing cursive swirls of blue;
green maple and beech leaves wiggle with delight
in the southern breeze, each indelibly exact;

and only a couple or three animal corpses lie
crumpled on the edge of the pavement like
cheap romances pulled from supermarket racks,
and once done with, of no more value, tossed
out windows and left to molder in the rain,
which is on the way—maybe by tonight,
tomorrow for sure. But tomorrow is tomorrow,
not now, not this beautiful day. Today I think
about my friend, wherever he is, if there is a wherever,
and I delight in what I know he would: that lately,
after years of what appeared to be a permanent absence,
woodchucks have been popping up along the Taconic,
one or two every few miles. Unlike his jokes,
which for me are evidently extinct, woodchucks,
those funny little waddlers, have made a comeback.
Here's to them, and him. Here's to what persists.

7. *Nothing Against Phil Ochs*

Okay, so I don't know Mingus from Monk,
Lester from Bird, Webster from Diz—
all that jazz. And one room-stinking stogie
is like any other, as far as I can tell.

He knew them all, this Havana and that,
the whole damned history of cigars.
And country music, too. That came after jazz,
midway between it and the Greek poets

he was so smitten by near the end, his study
of them inspired, he said, by the Cantos,
those nearly indecipherable poems that pound
for pound were true music if ever there was.

At the wake, though, Bob Dylan or Phil Ochs
was the ongoing argument, Ochs winning out:

his buddy John played one of Ochs' songs,
an anthem for the workers of this world.

The rabbi sang some generic prayers, in Hebrew.
So did Herb, another friend. I read two poems—
one his, one mine; his inspired by Callimachus,
a poem about the benefit of making love in a canoe,

mine about Bird playing his sax to a cow.
Both were brief, both funny. I didn't,
but had I thought of it, I would have played
a song I heard in Wicked Joe's Café

about a guy remembering the times when he
and a lover used to meet down by a river
and how he's sad those days, and I guess
the lover, are gone and won't be coming back

and how he's not now or ever will be the same;
which left me feeling like a drain so backed up
I thought I'd drown. Nothing against Phil Ochs,
but that's the song I would have played.

8. *Right Now*

In Wendell's Café, like the coffee, *Change is Good*.
It says so, someone having printed it in magic
marker-yellow on the black frame of a white door
under one of those geometrically arranged pop
paintings faintly reminiscent of *The Scream*
replete with swirls, triangles and straight lines;
diagonals of green, folds of red, blue, orange and yellow;
the crouching human figures a textural shade of white
once known as alabaster ghostly, more
alien-looking than human with nearly featureless faces,
heads hairless, eyes colorless slits, no mouths to scream.

Screams rise in me: *What platitudinous shit.*
I only think it, but things thought are just as real,
and change is not good, is not bad. Just is—
like birds, like bees, like snakes; like ashes, dust.
Change can't bring him back, or no change.
And even if I want to back up to before,
now will not let me, its reverse gear gone.
Forward's glacial, and only in the lowest gear.
Right now neutral is the best I can do.

9. Goodbye to Boyo

Give thanks, the preacher says, to the cosmos
God brought forth, and consequently you.
Give thanks to the earth on which you lived,
to the food you ate, to the air you breathed.

Give thanks to the pagoda built of wood
from a tree laid low, like Jericho, like you.
Give thanks to its replacement, the live oaks
shading the pallet on which you sat and you.

Give thanks to the wind flicking the leaves,
and to its flicking of candles and incense, too.
Give thanks to the holy rolling of cigars,
and to their residue of ashes and desire.

Give thanks to rafter-rockin' gospel, to jazz,
to country, and to the everlovin' blues.
Give thanks to BB's sultry 6-string riffs,
and to Bird's beboppin' sugar-daddy sax.

Give thanks, the preacher says, to all of these,
but most of all, give thanks to all like you
parsing out praise for the things of this world
worthy of praise. Oh, and we do, Boyo, we do.

10. *Closure? Did Somebody Say Closure?*

After he fled from the planet in plain view
of everybody in the bar in southeast Philly
on Bloomsday, I fled like a desperate Russian
on the run from the Mob north to New Hampshire.
But who was more desperate? I could say him,
but he's dead and I'm not; on the other hand,
he's safe, being dead. Or I could say me,
as I survive and he doesn't; on the other hand,
being alive, I'm still here and in their sights.
What really kills me, now he's as far away
as Kansas is from the ocean, is no matter
if it's north or south, east or west I run,
Kansas is where it is and it's my poor head
grief, that undying whore, is gunning for.

11. *The True Oblique: To a Fellow Harvester*

The image comes from Keats, but not the rhyme
you've used: that's Shakespeare, Wilfred Owen, too,
those vowels that slant like blackbirds over some
godawful field of stricken wheat Van Gogh,
as on fire as his vision was, would know
was equal to his crows. Of course, the rest
is pure Keats, down to the nightingales and ah!
that bitter chill that hammered at his breast
and left him doubting Fanny—Fanny, who,
like his riddled lungs, or Van Gogh's severed ear,
was merely convenient, pain, as he well knew,
cold beauty's harvest, not the softening, clear
nights of another April.
                          And, really, dear
friend, what is it we're talking of? Could you
have heard that thrush he said was coming near
as he lay in what you have called his Slough
of Despond, would you have thought of Fanny first—

those ample hips, those hands—or would you, too,
have disowned knowledge? Whether cursed or blessed
in thinking spring was harvest-time, as you
have named your crown of sonnets, Keats and time,
like glasses and weak eyes, like daft Van Gogh
and bloody shreds of ear, explain slant rhyme,
the true oblique—the yellow field, the crow.

The world approaches spring full tilt, but it's
spareness that grips—for instance, your one line
claiming shattered dreams of balance as your own—
and not the rhyme. The image comes from Keats.

Nude Man in the Water: The Poetry of David Dooley

Once there was Story Line Press. Then there wasn't. Now there is again—as an imprint of Red Hen Press. Once, too, there were two Story Line books, *The Volcano Inside* and *The Revenge by Love*. Then there wasn't, both out of print. Now there is again—both books just reissued as a single volume, *The Long Conversation*.

Here, I will limit myself to a consideration of *The Volcano Inside*. To *The Revenge by Love*, the second half of which is a sequence of poems that examines the art of Georgia O'Keeffe and her relationship with photographer Alfred Stieglitz, whatever critical points I make apply equally. What is true of one is true of both.

To begin, then, look closely at the following lines:

> Life, the old drag queen, takes off her wig, loosens her headband,
> revealing a wrinkled little man, ugly and silly.

Quite aside from the inherent pathos of the image, the mixed tone of irreverence and affection, and the aptly wrenched syntax, they are, in their totality of effect, simply wonderful. And any book that begins, as *The Volcano Inside* did in the 1988 first edition, with lines like the following has something going for it from the start:

> What the goddamn hell are you talking about, boy,
> I never did one thing in my life on account of a theory—
> look here: do you breathe theory? do you piss theory? do you fuck theory?

And in the case of David Dooley's *The Volcano Inside* there's more. Much more. And if there's any doubt, look at the last line in the book:

> Spare me the kvetching. Most of the night is still ahead of us.

A poet who can begin and end his book with lines like the above is not, one safely can assume, going to disappoint. Rather, the reader is going to be in the position of a man I know who found himself one morning at the center of the universe—the center according to Algonquin myth. Or was it Iroquois? In any event, the center was a pond in a park not far from Ithaca, New York.

There were four of us. We had hiked in, a mile or so along the public path, and were hot and sticky. Naturally the pond, with its small waterfall at the far end, was very inviting. But it was a public place and we hadn't any swimsuits. Three of us were deterred; one wasn't. "I'm going in," he said, locking his jaw in that way that says no argument allowed. Off came his shirt; off came his shoes, socks and pants; off came his underwear. And in he went. Half bemused and half embarrassed, we stood on shore and watched. No sooner was he in the water than voices sounded just around the nearest bend in the public path. Then they appeared: a man, a woman and two children—one a tot, the other a girl of about twelve or so. She was the first to round the bend into view, the pond opening to her like a geisha's delicate fan. She stopped dead in her tracks, gawked, turned to her parents and exclaimed: "Mommy! Daddy! There's a nude man in the water!"

Reading David Dooley's poems is like that. You stand on shore gawking like the girl, but soon you see it is yourself you're gawking at. *You* are the nude man in the water at the center of the universe. This is the way of all good art. And *The Volcano Inside* is very good art.

David Dooley is a retired legal assistant. He lives in San Diego but was born in Knoxville, Tennessee in 1947. He has two degrees, and *The Volcano Inside* was his first collection of poems, published in 1988. These are the facts.

Another fact is that David Dooley is one of those rare things today: a poet who has not had even one workshop; who is self-taught—so well, in fact, that he wrote an accomplished and uncompromising book. Winning awards doesn't, of course, necessarily establish or validate a poet. Often there's no relationship between the two. Dooley is an exception. *The Volcano Inside*, winner of the 1988 Nicholas Poetry prize, both established its author and was deserving of its award. These, too, are facts.

And so is this: Only the work itself can truly establish an author, and of the twenty-two poems included in the fifty pages of *The Volcano Inside* there are several that are unforgettable, each in its own distinctive way, and one that is masterly. Aptly, this poem is the first in the book; apt, because in its language, its technique, its form and its slant—its way of looking at the world—it sets itself as both exemplar of and commentator on all that follows, and in a most organic way. The language alone leaves the poem no choice.

This poem, titled "How I Wrote It," is a monolog in which, like Henry Miller, Dooley has transmuted what in lesser hands would be merely the outrageously obscene into high art. The language is gutsy, earthy and quixotic; the emotional and moral impulse, the *spiritus*, generous—that is to say, open, worldly in the wholesome sense. This generosity, more than anything, defines the art of David Dooley: the voices he assumes, the form; and the form, the *spiritus*; the generosity.

Look at the lines. They are long, swooping in and out, opening, breathing; are expansive, and explosive—like the language and the life force of the speaker. He is of the world—of Paris, of Marseilles, of Florence; of whores and drink and primal sex. And in his language he's American in the strutting, no-holds-barred and democratic way of Americans. He is a poet with the instincts of a bum. He wears women and sex like flesh, and when he asks, "Young man/ could your generation satisfy a whore?" we know the question is rhetorical. His "I doubt it" merely signs itself as such. The language, however, is the thing. It's scatological, slangy, racy, but, and here's the point, it's also poetry; it's the blood that races through his body, through his very being:

> What was it
> you said to me earlier, something about the form of the novel having failed
> so that only the not-novel could be the novel? Horseshit!
> Horseshit! It's the volcano inside you that has to erupt.
> The lava doesn't care where it burns. If the book is bleeding chunks
> so is life. The blood lets you recognize the source.

If this isn't both an aesthetic declaration and a rebuke to the aesthetics of negation, what is? To those *poseurs* who are so fond of asking "What came first, the theory or the poem?" the speaker's answer is forthright:

> There were no answers
> because there were never any questions. If you write,
> you don't need answers. That's where you fellows go wrong.

How wrong they've gone he specifies when he tells the "boy" to whom he's speaking in the poem,

> The novel, how to write the novel, I heard that guff
> in *caves*, bars, cafes, from writers who drank when
> they should have been writing, and some, as Prescott said,
> who wrote when they should have been drinking.

Immediately following this, he says that

> Writing means getting your hands dirty,
> writing means getting filthy all over. Holy men like dirt.

And there it is—*holy men*—. The sex, the seeming hedonism and depravity, the obscene language—all of this is nothing less than generation of the art. The writer, like the holy man, must tend his garden. And when he says,

> and while she slept,
> on summer nights the windows open and she lay there naked asleep
> the covers tangled down at her knees till I wouldn't know
> if I were writing with my pen or my cock,

he means it literally. The man is making love, but not only to Olga, "Polish whore and a damn good one"; not to "that Oriental whore"; not to Annele, whore whom "every writer in Paris wanted to bang...." He's "banging" and being banged by the Muse. And oh, what a bang it is! There is, in "How I Wrote It," a deeply good nature and good sense at work. This is reflected in the tone of voice, in the language, in the author's close attention to line and word, and in the real affection for life really lived that only a mature comedic sensibility, "that divinest of sounds, poet's laughter," can hope to communicate. All of these are abundantly on display in this poem and in Dooley's poems generally. Can we doubt it? Look at the last two lines:

> I knew how to live with the grime, you see.
> The grime on a tenement is as beautiful as the sunrise.

Some might not like the language; some might not like the animosity toward "theory" and its practitioners; some might not like even the speaker's wide-open sexuality. But most will smile at and admire a man who talks so flamboyantly and vulgarly and honestly about his art. Good humor and good sense expressed so lustily beget the same. Quite simply, the poem is illustration of what it talks about and contemplates. The poem becomes the symbol of itself. That is, the *idea* of the poem defines itself in the creation of the poem. If this is irony, given the dramatic context of an artist talking into a tape recorder about the context of his art, it's not just irony for its own sake. It pulls away the mask even as it insists on it.

Mask is important to this book. It opens with a monolog—a form in which the voice is mask—and closes with another, "Take Five." In the former we have the practitioner of one art for, the novel, talking about that art, and in the latter the practitioner of another, film, talking about it, or rather, demonstrating it through his direction of a group of actors. "This time I don't want to see quite so much imagination," he tells them, then, ironically, proceeds to demonstrate just that with real elan and gusto—mocking, coaxing, pleasing and revealing, always revealing, as the monolog must do. In Dooley's hands imagination is, as it should be, primary. Even the structure of the book shows this: all those "real" masks that are the other poems enclosed by two long poems in which the speakers talk about creating masks, i.e., their art.

Look, for example, at "The Reading," another wonderful poem in which a fortune teller, "fat and fifty," starts a session, and the poem, with "You see auras, do you not? No? You will, / and very soon," then becomes herself the aura that we see. "How I Wrote It," "Take Five," "The Reading": All three are monologs, poems of dramatic moments, poems of voice. And even in the smaller, more lyric poems the voice is always just off color, odd, disturbing and distinct. But, and here's another crucial point, you always have the feeling that these voices are invented, not just aspects of the author's own. In other words, this isn't merely one more confessional poetry. It is invented; it is fiction, imagination fired into high art.

And the voices this art takes:

> You have
> a highly spiritual nature, you want to
> float on the mystery of life like a boat on a still lagoon,

our unbowed fortune teller tells her client tenderly, through an exquisite, haunting simile.

One of those smaller lyric poems is the raunchy, funny "Johnson at 34"—Johnson, who goes for the jugular:

> Life will be great
> now that I've outlived Jesus.
> Today at school I should have opened the door,
> flung out my arms and said,
> "It's my birthday, I get to fuck any woman I want."
> Ten years ago today was one of the five best days
> of my life. I climbed a firetower in the Ozarks
> with Allen Ginsberg. We saw everything.
> I'll never forget it.
> Irish whiskey for dessert?
> It's my birthday, boy, and I love the taste.
> What do I want? I want to be great, fucked,
> famous, and loved, in that order.

If Johnson is the carnival barker of the heart, and he is, in another monolog, "Weasels Ripped My Flesh," the speaker is the grounds crew picking its way among the rubbish, the debris, left by the audience, trying to put things right. He is the "regional troubleshooter for a big corporation" who imagines himself in Hell and "screaming with all the rest," atoning for the sin of having only shown up "when there's something wrong, major wrong." The angel of death, he says, "They called me the angel of death," and lived up to it by handing out in one day 135 pink slips. And talk about irony, he thinks of himself as "part lawyer, part father, part priest," and says he'd tell them "part rabbi,/ but no one in Texas has ever heard of Jews,/ they just think I'm from New York and talk funny." Angel of death indeed. But notice, in this poem, as in so many others, art turns its lens on itself. Our lawyer (legal assistant?) says he has "this great idea for a short story," that

> maybe you could help me with the structure, a little symbolism
> here and there, et cetera. I figure it's good for a thousand words,

and ends, "How do you write a short story, anyway?" Humor aside, in its perhaps more overtly self-deprecatory way, this poem returns us to the tart putdowns in "How I Wrote It." No more than to theories can you write to quotas, schemes, technique. To write is to erupt. This is the only law. You break it at your peril.

Peril, however, is good for voice. No other event, either potential or experienced, thought of or felt, can so transfigure the language of a poem, giving its speaking voice such tones of urgency, such definition. And language, more than all their other virtues, is what so distinguishes the poems in *The Volcano Inside*; is what makes them boldly different from so much of what is being written now; is what makes them unforgettable and, clearly in the case of the ones cited here, so necessary. And what language! Colloquial, scatological, learned, lyric, allusive—each used smartly and, together, potently, a witch's brew of vowels and consonants and syllables and words and lines. In the torrent of Dooley's language all we can do is paddle, ride the flood, like the nude man in the water. Even in the slighter poems, and there's precious few, the language never slackens. In these the architecture, the skeleton, might be of modest size and strength, but the flesh, the language, always keeps its form, is always taut. Dooley's accrual of detail; his turning of phrase; his imagery ("the gulls flap above the waves like flying baby bottles"); his chosen moments of pure drama; his gothic sensibility—all these are, in his poems, accomplished, stunning, original. But language is the tenement of which these things are part. It's how the poet shapes, and is shaped by, the language that makes him a poet. Language is the poet's burden, and his love. And, as Dooley clearly knows, "the greater the love,/ the greater the burden."

The Volcano Inside, as well as *The Revenge by Love*, is a necessary book. It's necessary because, like all such books, it recognizes, as the fortune teller in "The Reading" does about her client, that

> For you the mind, and you have a good mind, is not enough,
> you want to press beyond the veils.

These poems allow us to do just that. They are, of course, rooted in "Life, the old drag queen," as poetry, of all the literary arts, supremely is; but in their rootedness they reach into the very center of the world, the universe, and blossom forth, transfiguring everything and pressing beyond those veils. And there, thanks to the gift that is the poem, we float, free of all shores, nude men and women in the water:

>   Come, then:
>   flex we must,
> and straighten, arc into sunlight, submerge into
> blue-brown murk, and sound our way upriver
> till we reach the source, confluence of jungle rains and mountain snows.

David Dooley, poet

What Students Need to Know about Syntax

"What is syntax?" That was my opening question to my Introduction to Poetry section one memorable first day of class. I will never forget the answer that came wafting in from the rear of the room: "A tax on sin!" At first I took it as a joke, but soon realized the student was absolutely serious. Syntax. It, and all aspects of grammar, bedevil many students today. Yet many of those same students fancy themselves as budding writers. Especially infamous is the would-be poet, convinced that all she has to do is sit and wait for the divine breath to enter her ear and all will be greatness and poetic light! That also is why the first thing I would do in almost every class I taught was to put a small poem up on the blackboard and spend an entire class period looking at nothing but the syntax: the constitution of the sentences and the elements and their placement within the sentence. "Syntax," I would say sternly, "means, literally, to put together, to arrange in order." Puffed up to my most glorious professorial splendor, "The word syntax," I would snap briskly, "comes from French from Late Latin from Greek." Then, like the master performer I was, I would spin, walk to the blackboard and carefully print the first stanza of a poem, rolling up my sleeves immediately after as a visual indicator of the work that was about to ensue:

> I placed a jar in Tennessee,
> And round it was, upon a hill.
> It made the slovenly wilderness
> Surround that hill.

Then the questions would begin. "Tell me," I say ominously, "what kind of sentencing does the poet use here, and why?" Dead silence. "Okay," I then prompt, "let's look at the first sentence. What type is it?" A hand timidly goes up. Acknowledged, the student asks haltingly,

"Isn't it a coordinating sentence?" Sweat breaks out on my upper lip. "Uh, well, "I say bemusedly, "you have the right idea but not the right term. Anyone?" Silence. Figuring a flank attack might work better, I move on, asking, "Is the second sentence the same type? If not, what's different?" Silence again, but not so extended this time. A voice shouts out excitedly, "The second sentence is all one part, but the first has two parts!" I almost faint from the rush of adrenaline that comes with this small victory. Now it is time for the second part of the question: Why? Why is the first sentence a bit more complicated? And what does it allow the poet to emphasize? Half a dozen hands shoot up. Ah, I think, we are making progress. "Because," one student says elatedly, "there are two different things being shown in the first sentence, and only one in the second." A pause. "Yes," I urge, "and what are they exactly?" The student wrinkles his brow in deep concentration. Then his whole face lights up. "In the first sentence," he explains triumphantly, "the guy describes how he places the jar in the first line, and in the second describes the shape of the jar and where it is." I have to restrain myself from running over and hugging the kid! Now for the ultimate test. "Why," I ask, "do you think the poet has that rather archaic expression, 'And round it was'"? The silence lengthens like the late afternoon sunlight coming through the Venetian blinds. I am very near despair once more when, unbelievably, the answer comes: "Because he wants to stress the roundness of the jar." I can no longer contain myself, and "Yes!" I virtually screech, jumping up and down. "Yes!" Of course it will only get more difficult in the days and weeks ahead, but for now, for this one moment, they deserve a pat on the back. And so do I. "Class dismissed!" I bellow. They look at the clock and then at me with what appears to be real affection, realizing I am letting them out ten whole minutes early. Thus ends the first crucial lesson in syntax. There is hope after all.

Acknowledgments

Atticus Review: "Lingering Sweetness: On the Road with George" (under the title "Lingering Sweetness: The Essays of Paul Ruffin"); *Easy Street Magazine*: "I Beg You, Ezra," "What Students Most Need to Know About Syntax: A Mini-Essay"; *Literary Matters (ALSCW)*: "Lodging a Poem"; *Louisiana Literature*: "Just Like Oz: The Making of a Book"; *Madville Publishing* (website): "Of Puffery"; *The Main Street Rag*: "Crazy Dance: What Actually is Being Said in Father/Son Poems"; *Schuylkill Valley Journal*: "What Makes a Poem a Master Work?"; *The Texas Review*: "Fixing the Shimmer: The Hard Art of Poetry," "Poems that Jack Took: The Dressing Down of an Editor"; *Valley Voices*: "Nude Man in the Water: The Poetry of David Dooley"

Grateful thanks to the editors, especially to Kimberly Davis, Jack Bedell and the late Paul Ruffin, who consistently encouraged and supported me as a poet and sometimes essayist and reviewer.

Thanks also to Jared Smith and Jack Butler, for their wonderful work, inspiration and friendship; and to the late Martin Ludwig and Harry Staley, the two most important teachers in my life.

About the Author

GEORGE DREW is the author of nine poetry collections, including *Pastoral Habits: New and Selected Poems* and *The View from Jackass Hill*, winner of the 2010 X.J. Kennedy Poetry Prize, both from Texas Review Press, *Fancy's Orphan*, Tiger Bark Press, and most recently *Drumming Armageddon*, Madville Publishing, 2020. Drew also has published a chapbook, *So Many Bones: Poems of Russia*. He has a new chapbook coming out titled *Hog: A Delta Memoir*, Bass Clef Press. He has won awards such as the South Carolina Review Poetry Prize, the Paumanok Poetry Award, the Adirondack Literary Award, the St. Petersburg Review Poetry Contest, the Knightville Poetry Contest and in 2020 the William Faulkner Literary Competition. Drew was a recipient of the Bucks County Muse Award in 2016 for contributions to the Bucks County, Pennsylvania, literary community. His biography appears in *Mississippi Poets: A Literary Guide*, University of Mississippi Press, edited by Catherine Savage Brosman. In 2019, Drew collaborated with singer/songwriter Rick Kunz on a CD of original poetry and songs entitled *A Triumph of Loneliness*, KBW Music.

www.ingramcontent.com/pod-product-compliance
Lightning Source LLC
Chambersburg PA
CBHW030116170426
43198CB00009B/639